LOVING GOD'S MASTERPIECE

Seven Strategies to Rebuilding Your Self-Esteem and Self-Image

Lakeytha G. Clayton

Loving God's Masterpiece: Seven Strategies to Rebuilding Your Self-Esteem and Self-Image

© 2018 Lakeytha G. Clayton

ISBN: 978-0-692-14337-7

First Printing 2018

Sparkle Publishing Company
www.sparklepublishing.net

Editor: Sharp Editorial, LLC (Laci Swann)
Cover Design: Zak Arianada

All biblical references are used from the New Living Translation (NLT) ©

Contents

Dedication

This book is dedicated to my only daughter, Eryka Chanelle Clayton. I am so proud of the young lady you are becoming. As you continue to grow, I hope you will embrace who you are in Christ and all He created you to be in this world. My prayer is that this book will one day benefit you as you continue to live in His image and through all He has created you to become. There is no limit to what you can do with God on your side. I love you and ALWAYS remember – you are a MASTERPIECE.

Acknowledgments

First, I must acknowledge God who gave me life and the vision for this book. Without Him being the Head of my life, I would not be here today, in this moment.

Thank you to the man who has been in my life for over 17 years and by my side in marriage for over 15 years, Eric Clayton. Eric, thank you for your unwavering support through all of my endeavors. You motivate me to be a better woman and a better wife. I love you more than I will ever be able to verbally and physically demonstrate, always and forever.

Thank you to my two heartbeats, Eryka and Caleb. Thank you for praying for me and challenging me to be the best mother I can be to each of you. I love you to pieces.

Also, a special thanks to my brother, Anthony Guillory, Jr., who has served as my spiritual advisor and prayer partner from the very beginning of this project.

Preface

It was the night of May 22, 2010, my sister's wedding day. My little sister just married the love of her life, and I should have felt ecstatic, right?

The truth is, I put every ounce of energy I had into putting a mere smile on my face that evening. I mustered up the strength to fake my way through her beautiful ceremony, a ceremony I should have felt elated to witness.

The clock struck 11, and I found myself looking in the bathroom mirror, disgusted at my reflection. I saw a pitiful, pathetic, overweight woman. I saw a woman who could not stand to be in her own skin.

As I looked in the mirror, tears began to flow, tears I had been holding back, all evening, to avoid a breakdown on my little sister's special day.

As I looked at the woman staring back at me, a woman I thought was full of flaws, I could not help but think about the remarks that relatives had made, earlier that evening, regarding my weight gain.

What happened to you?!

You got so big!

Wow, you put on weight!

Replaying those remarks tipped off a long, toxic conversation in my mind of everything that was wrong with me and my life.

Without saying a word to anyone at the wedding, nor telling my husband where I was going, I frantically hopped in my car and began driving. To where, I didn't know. Moments later, I started to scream hysterically, crying, beating my fists against the steering wheel, losing all control of my emotions. I had no idea where I was going, but I knew I wanted to escape reality and fast.

I finally came to a stop about 20 miles away from my home. I parked my car in the parking lot of a random hotel, and I sat for what felt like an eternity, crying my eyes out. I was hysterical. I hated myself. I despised the woman I had become. I drove with the unrealistic expectation of escaping from the very person I could not avoid. Although I drove to another city that evening, I could not get away from the person who was making my life miserable – me. I could not escape the disgust, and I could not break away from the woman causing me to quickly spiral into a world of low self-esteem and poor self-image. *I was my own worst enemy.*

As I sat in that desolate hotel parking lot, I wrestled with thoughts of suicide. I thought, perhaps, if I left the world, I would no longer feel pain and torment. As I continued to think about making a permanent escape, an image popped into my mind, a sudden, beautiful reminder of the three people I could never turn my back on – my family.

I decided to put an end to my thoughts of suicide and return home in one piece. My mind and heart were in shambles, yet God was the driving force behind my safe return home to my family. And so I returned home, yet I continued to battle with myself. I was tired. I knew this destructive mode of thinking and feeling had to stop.

***

As I sit here, writing this book, I am in awe as to how I have reached the point of comfortably and confidently sharing my story. I have always been a private individual, taught that what occurs in your home must remain in your home. Needless to say, sharing details, experiences, and life struggles is a major progression. However, it is imperative I remain transparent and address issues that many women face on a daily basis, issues that women face but are embarrassed, ashamed, or afraid to openly discuss, issues that have left women feeling empty and broken. I know what it is like to experience pain and inner turmoil, feeling as if I was the only one fighting a battle while viewing others moving forward and experiencing success.

By the grace of God, I have several testimonies of God's power in my life. I am truly a miracle, and although, for length's sake, I cannot share all that has transpired in my life in one book, I am humbled to provide an honest glimpse of what my life has been like and the obstacles I have overcome. In previous years, different individuals planted the seed in my mind that I should write a book and praise God in written form, and I have reached the season in my life where God has released me to do just that. I thank Him for this appointed time, and I pray my story impacts women around the world, women with an obscured level of self-esteem and self-image, viewing themselves as anyone less than God's child. Upon reading the last word of this book, my desire is that you will be on the right path to recognizing that you are not just an ordinary woman, but God's masterpiece for whom He has a good plan for your life.

"For we are God's masterpiece. He has created us anew in Christ Jesus, so we can do the good things he planned for us long ago."

(Ephesians 2:10)

Introduction

Self-esteem is shaped by a person's thoughts, relationships, and experiences. The way a person feels about him or herself, and how they regard their abilities and limitations, contributes to self-esteem. People exhibit one of two levels of self-esteem: healthy self-esteem and low self-esteem. Healthy self-esteem occurs when an individual feels good about him or herself, believing he or she is deserving of respect. Low self-esteem occurs when an individual places little value on his or her opinions and ideas, continuously worrying if he or she is good enough.

Self-image, although in the same family as self-esteem, differs in meaning. Self-image is a mental picture depicting details such as height, weight, and hair color but also includes learned behaviors. Self-image is determined by personal experiences or internalizing the judgments of others. The answer one would give that defines a person's self-image is based on the question, "What do you believe people think about you?" Furthermore, poor self-image may result from accumulated criticisms one received as a child. Accumulated criticisms often lead to a damaged self-image. How a woman views herself and assesses her value will play a major role in how successful she will be in life. Your level of self-esteem and self-image will be factors in what you accomplish, professionally and personally. This book is dear to my heart because I share former struggles and experiences revolving around my battle with low self-esteem and poor self-image. Additionally, I will share effective strategies for reprograming your thought process.

***

At some point in a woman's life, she has experienced dissatisfaction with herself, whether over a minor issue or a major issue. Experiencing doubt or discontent is normal; however, when dissatisfaction becomes continually present, it begins to interfere with your self-esteem and self-worth. Low self-esteem and poor self-image involve comparing yourself to other women, continuously focusing on your weaknesses, imperfections, shortcomings, flaws, and feelings of stagnancy:

She is so much prettier than I am.

Her family seems much happier than mine.

I wish I had her job.

I will never be as successful as her.

I am a testimony of how God can and will help you re-invent yourself as a woman, reprograming your thinking as it relates to your self-esteem and self-image.

Loving God's Masterpiece is an account of my journey of rebuilding my self-esteem and self-image. I know, first-hand, the toll that low self-esteem and poor self-image can take on a person, mentally, physically, emotionally, and spiritually. In this book, I share faith-based tactics that have allowed me to successfully transition from feeling utterly disgusted with myself to whole-heartedly believing I am a *masterpiece,* created by God, fearfully and wonderfully made. These positive tactics continue to be in motion in my life today as I successfully maintain and exceed my levels of self-love.

This book will address the mental, physical, emotional, and spiritual aspect that creates your entire being as a woman, including your strengths, gifts, and talents. I will share how my mind was transformed, how I began to recognize my beauty, how I celebrated my strengths, and how I continue to maintain my self-confidence and self-worth. As you read about my journey, you will understand that my faith and personal relationship with God are the driving forces providing the strength to maintain my self-esteem and self-image.

As women, we fulfill different roles. We come from various walks of life and socioeconomic backgrounds. In spite of our many differences, we share a special commonality – the desire to live our best possible life. My name is Lakeytha G. Clayton, and this is my story, *Loving God's Masterpiece.*

Strategy #1: Fearfully and Wonderfully Made

God has blessed me to arrive at a point in my life where I not only like myself, but I love myself. I have an awesome testimony of how God transformed my thought process as it relates to my self-image. Transforming my mind and heart, arriving at the point of joy and contentment, has taken years of trials, tribulations, mistakes, tears, prayers, and learned wisdom. God has been so good to me that I felt it was imperative to share my story regarding His unconditional love, grace, mercy, and goodness. *"Give thanks to the Lord, for He is good; His loves endures forever"* (Psalms 136:1).

When I finally decided to write a book, revealing my life struggles, experiences, and lessons, I had no idea where to begin, which was a fantastic problem to have because I realized I have so much that God has seen me through. So, not knowing where to start was yet another blessing in disguise. His deliverance has been *that* profound! Nevertheless, He is always on time because at that moment, when I realized I could and should write my first book, God immediately provided a focus of which I should share my story with my fellow sisters. For many years, I secretly struggled with low self-esteem and a negative self-image. Those debilitating thoughts and harmful feelings began as a child and, unfortunately, carried over into womanhood, permeating my feelings regarding my special roles as wife and mother.

From my teenage years to my early thirties, I experienced feelings no woman or man of God should endure. I was overcome with severe levels of disgrace for who I had become. I could not look at myself in the mirror without my mind conjuring negative thoughts, which eventually spewed out of my mouth.

You are not pretty!

You are too skinny!

You are too fat!

You are not smart enough!

You don't have any talents!

You are a horrible wife!

You are weak and pathetic!

You can't do anything right!

Imagine hearing those statements in your mind, repeatedly, over an extended period. The results are devastating. Over time, I lost appreciation for the *masterpiece* God created. I had little appreciation for myself and all that I had to offer when, in fact, I should have been looking at myself through the eyes of the Most High: *"For we are God's masterpiece. He has created us anew in Christ Jesus, so we can do the good things he planned for us long ago"* (Ephesians 2:10).

Instead of recognizing the respected work of art He purposefully created, the *masterpiece,* the treasure, and a gem of God, I had come to believe I was a failure and, worse, an absolute disgrace, certainly not viewing myself as a *masterpiece.* I did not feel that I was fearfully and wonderfully made. My low self-esteem and poor self-image had become a stronghold, dictating every facet of my adult life.

My battle with low self-esteem and poor self-image began early at ten years old. I vividly remember the degrading thoughts I had about myself, and I struggled with that same debilitating battle into adulthood. This back and forth, abusive, inner dialogue was a negative, recurring cycle, an emotional roller coaster with no end in sight. My low self-esteem involved psychosocial issues, emotional issues, physical issues, and spiritual issues.

In July 2010, I finally hit rock bottom with this recurring cycle. I had a severe psychotic breakdown which resulted in my admission to a psychiatric program and a six-month sabbatical from my career as a social worker.

Self-esteem and self-image play vital roles in the success of your life, and success is not simply confined to professional success. Self-esteem is vital for emotional success, spiritual strength, and so forth. The impact of self-esteem and self-image can be seen as early as preschool age. A three or four-year-old child understands the weight of being praised and applauded. Additionally, when encouraged, children typically want to continue the positive display of behavior to continue receiving praise or rewards. Children want to continuously demonstrate what they can do because they enjoy hearing that he is a "good boy" or she is a "good girl." These positive acknowledgments show approval, consequently building their self-esteem or self-image as well as confidence. Positive reinforcement and repetition is important at that age and continues to be important well into adulthood.

Your level of self-esteem is a catalyst to what you accomplish in life. Self-esteem is interchangeable with confidence, self-respect, self-satisfaction, and self-worth. Self-esteem motivates you to do better and become better if your self-esteem is at a healthy level. Exhibiting positive and healthy self-esteem motivates you to be productive, thriving throughout life. As an adult, you are in charge of your level of self-esteem and self-image, whether you have low self-esteem or a positive self-image. Individuals may belittle you or put you down but, ultimately, you must choose whether or not to allow those remarks to become embedded in your mind or leave with the changing of the wind. I recommend the latter.

Recognizing your value and worth is of the utmost importance but, more importantly, you must believe that your worth is important to God.

We are His masterpieces, ladies!

Am I fearfully and wonderfully made?

Yes, I am, according to Psalm 139:14: *"Thank you for making me so wonderfully complex! Your workmanship is marvelous – how well I know it."*

Before God formed you in the womb, He knew you! He knew the traits and characteristics unique to you and only you, characteristics that set you apart from anyone else. There is no one else molded like you, an intentional act of God on your behalf, which is the ultimate reason to not only remember your worth but also walk in your worth.

Not only do I like myself, but I love myself, a powerful feeling every man, woman, and child should feel. At the age of 38, I walk with my head held high, and I find indescribable joy and peace knowing I am made by The Creator. I am ecstatic about being the woman God has allowed me to develop into, exhibiting the strengths, qualities, and talents He fashioned for me and only me. Satan's mission is to have you believe that you do not equate to much, if anything at all, as well as believing that you may not amount to much of anything in the future. The devil wants to infiltrate your spirit with doubt, sadness, and confusion, especially by reminding you of your past, your pitfalls, your shortcomings, and areas of improvement. However, your past does not have to dictate your future. It is never too late to transform your low self-esteem and poor self-image, but transforming your self-worth will be a process. I pray this book assists you with the process, facilitating your decision and respective steps towards the level of self-love you deserve to feel.

If you have an issue or concern with any facet of your life, do something about it, especially if those issues can be fixed within your power.

Do you think raising or reviving your self-esteem cannot be done at your age?

Think again!

God specializes in making the impossible possible!

I live by that motto.

There is absolutely nothing on this Earth too difficult for God to tackle and conquer, absolutely nothing!

God is omnipresent (everywhere).

God is omniscient (all-knowing).

God is omnipotent (all-powerful).

God is all of those attributes built into one. Can you tell I am excited about the qualities of God? His abilities are awe-inspiring, perfect, and everlasting!

You must love who you were created to be, living your life to the fullest and with joy. You are royalty, a daughter of the Most High. As your fellow sister, I stand with you, praising God with you and for you. I encourage you to love yourself as God's masterpiece, living your life as a fearfully and wonderfully made woman.

Before He Formed You

Life begins at conception, but God knew you before you were conceived. Isn't that amazing? Yes, you were produced by the physical union of your mother and father, but God is your Creator:

And now the Lord speaks – the one who formed me in my mother's womb to be his servant, who commissioned me to bring Israel back to him. The Lord has honored me, and my God has given me strength

(Isaiah 49:5).

Psalms 139:13-16 tells you that God formed the way you think and feel. He put you together in your mother's womb. We praise Him because He made us in such a wonderful way. He knew how amazing you were! He could see your bones grow as your body took shape, hidden in your mother's womb. He could see your body grow in each passing day. You are engraved in the palm of God's hands, and you are always before His eyes (Isaiah 49:16). God knew how you would be formed, when you would be formed, and how you would turn out once you were formed. He knew who you would be today, and He knows who you will be in the future: *"But even before I was born, God chose me and called me by his marvelous grace. Then it pleased him"* (Galatians 1:15). God knows the most intimate details of your life. He knew what your innermost secrets would be before they transpired or developed. As you grow in stature, He continues to know every detail of your existence. God knows your innermost thoughts and feelings. When you experience feelings of hurt, fear, anger, or loneliness, He is hardly surprised. He knows why you shed tears, even when you cannot explain why you are sad. *Women can be complicated and complex, puzzling mankind, but a woman will never be too complicated or complex for God to decipher.* God is in tune with all of your struggles. No matter where you are in your life, at this very moment, God knows all about the situation and circumstances, and He knows you. And because He knows all about you, He knows how to mend your brokenness. Because He created you with intention and purpose, He will always know the result and every detail in between.

Priceless

Because you are God's masterpiece and fearfully and wonderfully made, you are deemed a treasure in the eyes of God. Gold and silver are commodities with high value, but you, my dear, are priceless, created in the very image of God. No value can be placed on your life, no price tag or tangible amount. You were not meant to be purchased or sold. However, when women want to feel loved or valued, they will often pay a high price to obtain those desires.

My heart deeply aches to know that women resort to selling their bodies, placing a number value on their priceless life.

My heart deeply aches to know women do not recognize their worth as human beings.

My heart deeply aches to know that human sex trafficking is rampant across the world, that young girls and women, as well as young boys and men, are being sold as sex slaves, having their God-given bodies abused or mistreated.

If these upsetting notions hurt my heart, you can imagine how God feels as your Creator. Your life means so much to God because you were created in His image. Recognize your value and worth as a woman, as a masterpiece.

You must realize, as God's masterpiece, that you are a priceless gift to humanity, too. It does not matter what your parents may have said to demean you, what your grade school teacher said to embarrass you, or what an abusive spouse or boyfriend said to degrade you, you are priceless in the eyes of God. Always remember – no amount of money can purchase your mind, body, and soul, either.

"And yet, O Lord, you are our Father. We are the clay, and you are the potter. We are all formed by your hand"

(Isaiah 64:8).

List the qualities that make you unique, qualities that make you being fearfully and wonderfully made:

_____

_____

_____

_____

_____

_____

_____

_____

_____

_____

_____

_____

_____

_____

_____

_____

_____

_____

_____

_____

_____

_____

Strategy #2: The Mental Transformation

As I discussed earlier, I remember battling low self-esteem and self-image issues as early as 10 years old. For the first eleven years of my life, I grew up in a home where I witnessed domestic violence. I remember walking on eggshells, attempting to not say or do anything that would upset my father. I developed the mentality that I had to be "good" in order to avoid his verbal or physical wrath. Being "good" included doing everything he stated to do when he wanted it done and how he wanted it done. For years, I walked on eggshells in an attempt to achieve perfection. At the age of 13, my parents divorced. Shortly after their divorce, my father moved out of the state. My relationship with him, as well as my siblings' relationship with him, became estranged. From that point forward, I began to live with feelings of rejection and abandonment. I began to question his love for me because he did not take the proper measures to remain part of my life or my siblings' lives. He just left. As I went through high school, I excelled in academics and felt great joy in not only being respected by my teachers and peers, but shining in the classroom, academically speaking. I was always an honor student. I was a member of the Beta Club, National Honor Society, and 4-H Club. I took honors courses, and I excelled in English. I have always loved reading and writing. Academics were an avenue to cope with and redirect my feelings of rejection and abandonment. Excelling in academics was a way to feel valued. After high school, I went to college and graduated with an associate degree in science from Louisiana State University. Two years later, I received a bachelor's degree in social work from Northwestern State University. Immediately after receiving my bachelor's degree, I attended Louisiana State University and earned my master's degree, also in social work, graduating summa cum laude. After earning those degrees and receiving praise from my loved ones, I continued to experience feelings of worthlessness.

Achieving academic success was a wonderful feeling, but nothing compared to meeting the love of my life in Houston, Texas, in July 2001. On January 4, 2003, I married the man I fell in love with, and two and a half years later, I gave birth to our first child, Eryka Chanelle. As I began to function in my roles as wife and mother, my self-esteem and self-image issues became increasingly evident. Although I had married the man I loved, the first five years of our marriage were extremely challenging. After six months of marriage, my husband shared the surprising news that God had called him into ministry. Not only was I still learning how to be a wife, but now I had the added stress of learning how to be a minister's wife. By January 2007, I was expecting our second child, and my husband was fully engaged in ministry. I felt the pressures of being a young ministry wife and a mother of two small children, working a full-time, stressful job as a social worker, and residing in a city without the support of any immediate family members.

During my second pregnancy, depression began to manifest. The year of 2007 began my mental roller coaster ride. That year was the first year my mental illness was diagnosed by a professional, and I came to the realization that I was mentally unstable. In retrospect, the first signs of depression appeared during my first trimester of my first pregnancy, but my feelings were mild, and I assumed that my mental disturbances were due to being pregnant. However, the real mental battle began in April 2007, while four months pregnant with my second child, resulting in my first encounter with a psychiatrist and an introduction to antidepressants. I had no idea this was the commencement of a long road of mental illness. July 2008 marked the beginning of being in and out of psychiatric hospitals and programs, psychotherapy sessions, a variety of prescribed antidepressants and antipsychotics, and an accelerated decline of self-esteem and self-image. I lived with feelings of despair, hopelessness, anger, fear, failure, loneliness, shame, guilt, and inadequacy. As I went through cycles of highs and lows, I battled with thoughts of suicide. I lived with mental torment, feeling as though I was being punished by God for whatever reason. Amid living with mental illness, I continued to receive love and support from my husband, mother, stepfather, siblings, and close church members (whom I had allow into my world of mental illness). However, their love and support did not eliminate the troublesome feelings I harbored. I experienced negative emotions and feelings despite being a born-again, spirit-filled believer. The fact that I had a relationship with Christ, ironically, exacerbated the negative opinions I had of myself. I could not comprehend how one could confess salvation and be filled with the Holy Spirit yet feel disgust and self-hatred. I constantly wondered, "Where was God and why was He allowing this to happen to me?" My husband constantly assured me that this dark period of my life had a purpose. I constantly questioned what that purpose could be because there was no way I could see beyond my despair.

My last admission to a psychiatric program was in July 2010, but I continued to ride my roller coaster of mental instability until the end of 2013. One evening, in February 2014, while watching a Joyce Meyer program, God began to transform my mind, as though Joyce Meyer was speaking directly to me through the television screen and knew my innermost thoughts. This mental transformation was the beginning of a new thought process. In that very moment, I began to recognize my value and worth as a woman, realizing who I was in Christ as a woman, wife, and mother. That night was the commencement of a new journey in my mind. It was the commencement of my mental transformation. I became a regular viewer of Joyce Meyer programs and began to read her books to assist in the strengthening of my mind. God's wisdom, love, and guidance were reaching me through Joyce Meyer, as she is a special vessel in communicating His Word, and so I began to retrain my mind, self-image, and self-esteem. I grew tired of being a "victim" and throwing pity parties. The time had come to get myself together, so I shifted my focus. I began to focus on what I *did* have going for me and what was going right in life. I began to make the shift from feeling disgusted and disappointed to believing in myself! I began to change my outlook on life, and I realized that I wanted to live my life in peace. I began to develop a sincere spirit of gratitude and appreciation for how far I had come. I began to thank and praise God for the smallest blessings, especially the overlooked blessings such as having an anxiety-free day, and I was so grateful. The acknowledgement of the smallest blessings gave me glimpses of hope. I made a conscious effort to stop complaining. I began to realize that I had to live for me and appreciate the life God had given me. My focus shifted from "poor me" to "I want to become the best me!" I began to focus on being comfortable in my skin and doing what was important to me, working to eradicate my fear of what others may think. I began focusing on becoming the best wife and mother. I began to release the worries of wondering what people were thinking and how I was viewed in the eyes of others. I began to journal and document the positive thoughts and events occurring in my life. I developed a prayer list of what I wanted to come to pass in my life. I developed a list of all my positive traits. I developed a list of positive behaviors I wanted to repeat, and I developed negative behaviors I wanted to remove. I began to make positive statements to myself about myself. I smiled more. I laughed more. I focused on strengthening my relationship with God and my husband and taking care of two young lives who needed a happy, healthy mother. I am a living witness that you can change, but you must put in the work.

The Power of Changing Your Words

"The tongue can bring death or life; those who love to talk will reap the consequences" (Proverbs 18:21). Proverbs 18:21 is one of my favorite scriptures. We often speak, not realizing the impact of what we are saying.

Words are powerful.

Words can tear down and destroy.

Words can build up and exalt.

This includes the words you feed your spirit. Therefore, you must be mindful of what comes out of your mouth concerning your life. If you change your words, you can change your life for the better.

Once upon a time, I spoke negatively regarding what was going on in my life, and I predicted my future with a negative connotation.

"You will battle mental illness for the rest of your life."

"You will always be in and out of psychiatric units."

"You are crazy."

"Nothing ever goes right!"

"You will never be 'normal.'"

Speaking negatively became my norm. As a result, I expected the worst, trying to prepare myself for trouble down the road. I often expected the worst possible outcome, and sometimes, I would receive what I expected. Often, I would suspect that my "good days" of not dealing with a debilitating episode of depression would be short-lived, and they often were temporary. I could go several months without an admission to a psychiatric program, and then I would have to be readmitted due to my inability to consistently manage and handle responsibilities such as trying to raise two small children, having a husband in ministry, working in a stressful professional arena, finance struggles, and so forth. Additionally, I was still dealing with "daddy" issues. I could not handle stress, and when life became too much, I would check out and shut down. I had a difficult time processing daily events, which is a symptom of depression. I would be ineffective in doing my job as a social worker. My medications were constantly being changed or adjusted when it seemed they were not properly managing my symptoms. I basically sat around and waited for the next episode. My cycle of being in and out of psychiatric programs became a way of life. I would often expect to have to take a medical leave of absence from my job due to my mental state, and the episode would eventually come to pass. I began to accept that my husband and I would continue to struggle with finances. Trying to make ends meet had become the norm, and I did not expect that to change. I could never see the good, but I had become an expert in speaking and expecting bad.

The Power of God's Word

The power of words is undeniable, but there are no words you could ever speak that will compare to the Word of God. Scripture lets you know that God's words do not leave your mouth and return without results. God's Word makes things happen that He wants to happen. His Word succeeds in doing what He sent His Words to do (Isaiah 55:11). One of my favorites scriptures is Ephesians 3:20: *"Now all glory to God, who is able, through his mighty power at work within us, to accomplish infinitely more than we might ask or think."* Another powerful scripture is found in Psalm 37:5: *"Commit everything you do to the Lord. Trust him, and he will help you."* These passages serve as perfect reminders never to underestimate the power of God's Word!

As I began to undergo my mental transformation, I realized I needed to dive into the Word of God. I had read the Word of God but, I admit, not as consistently as I should have and, at times, reading His Word was difficult to understand and retain. I invested in study Bibles and tools that would assist me in breaking down the scriptures. I did not want to merely read the Word of God for the sake of reading, but I wanted to understand His Word in such a way that I could make the scriptures applicable to my daily life. I became more passionate about the Word of God and its relevance in my life. I have come to learn that there is *always* a Word from God that can be aligned with anything I may face, including emotional turmoil and confusion. Declare the Word of God over your mental state and thought process. Repeat the words: "I am a child of God, and I have a sound mind. I am bold, fearless, and confident." A powerful scripture to declare, in addition to reciting the above-mentioned affirmation, is 2 Timothy 1:7: *"For God has not given us a spirit of fear and timidity, but of power, love, and self-discipline."*

God's Word can bring life to your self-esteem and self-image, reversing what Satan has planted in your mind.

The Word of God is sharper than any two edged sword.

The Word of God can free you from the same thoughts that hold you captive.

The Word of God can release you from mental anguish.

Deliverance will come with continuous study and repetition of God's Word. It does not matter what thoughts of inadequacy or insecurity that Satan or other people have placed in your mind. The only thing that matters is what the Word of God says about you. According to the Word, you are God's handiwork, created in Christ Jesus to do good works, which God prepared in advance for you to do (Ephesians 2:10). I challenge you to study God's Word and allow His opinion of you, as His masterpiece, to soak in your mind and heart. I encourage you to declare and decree His Word and promises over your mind. Boldly recite these words on a daily basis:

I am a masterpiece and God's handiwork. I am all God has created me to be. I will live for today and focus on matters of today. Today is the day that the Lord has made, and I will be glad!

Overcoming Mental Strongholds

Strongholds are areas of resistance to the Will of God. Low self-esteem and poor self-image are areas of your being that have been invaded and occupied by Satan. Self-esteem and self-image issues begin with what appear to be small, innocent thoughts or statements, or so you think, but develop and intensify with time. For instance, I would constantly condemn myself because I felt I did not have any real talents, and I would often believe I did not know how to do anything exciting or important. As time passed, this destructive thought became part of my reality, and those words led me to constantly compare myself to other women. Additionally, this mentality led me to believe that something was wrong with me. I would also tell myself that I did not know how *not* to worry. Let me tell you, constantly worrying became my norm. My worrying ways became extreme, to the point of making myself sick, which resulted in stomach aches and severe migraines. Strongholds are forms of bondage. Bondage, the state of being subjected to the control of external power, includes slavery to negative thoughts. The negative thoughts you have of yourself can dominate and influence your speech and actions.

Low self-esteem and poor self-image distort your beliefs. Distorted beliefs cripple and hinder your spiritual and natural life. Strongholds of your mental state cause you to become easy prey for Satan's use. As I battled with low self-esteem and poor self-image, along with self-pity, those negative modes of living and thinking became part of my innermost being. Those strongholds took over my life, but I praise God for deliverance. He can deliver you, too!

There is one stipulation to being delivered from any stronghold that may be consuming you – *the desire and commitment to change must be present.*

God does not and will not force you to do anything. He gives you free will. You must possess the sincere desire to be released from the bondage of your negative self-image. Become determined to defeat the enemy! Fight for what is rightfully yours as a *masterpiece* which is the ability to live with a sound mind.

Your Secret Place

Psalms 91:1-6, one of my favorite passages, reminds me I am safe in the arms of God:

Those who live in the shelter of the Most High will find rest in the shadow of the Almighty. This I declare about the Lord: He alone is my refuge, my place of safety; he is my God, and I trust him. For he will rescue you from every trap and protect you from deadly disease. He will cover you with his feathers. He will shelter you with his wings. His faithful promises are your armor and protection. Do not be afraid of the terrors of the night, nor the arrow that flies in the day. Do not dread the disease that stalks in darkness, nor the disaster that strikes at midday. Though a thousand fall at your side, though ten thousand are dying around you, these evils will not touch you. Just open your eyes, and see how the wicked are punished. If you make the Lord your refuge, if you make the Most High your shelter, no evil will conquer you; no plague will come near your home. For he will order his angels to protect you wherever you go. They will hold you up with their hands so you won't even hurt your foot on a stone. You will trample upon lions and cobras; you will crush fierce lions and serpents under your feet! The Lord says, "I will rescue those who love me. I will protect those who trust in my name. When they call on me, I will answer; I will be with them in trouble. I will rescue and honor them. I will reward them with a long life and give them my salvation.

When I used to struggle with reigning in my negativity, I learned that locating a quiet place to seek God's strength was helpful. I happen to have a "secret place" where God and I meet, a place where I can retreat when I need to have time alone with God. My secret place allows me to share my innermost thoughts and desires. My secret place has been my place of tranquility. Having a secret place played a major role in God transforming my life, and it continues to serve a great purpose because my place of retreat facilitates and encourages an ongoing relationship with quietude and stillness as I read God's Word and spend time in prayer. My secret place is where I can go to meditate on His Word, allowing Him to speak to me and comfort me. When I leave my secret place, I feel refreshed, mentally and spiritually. The way I spend time in my secret place depends on how I am doing at that moment. I shed tears, I offer praise, I meditate and reflect, and I do whatever the Holy Spirit leads me to do. I feel peace in my secret place because God is always there, waiting to receive me and give instructions.

I encourage you to create a secret place. This designated space may be your car, the bathroom, a closet, or another area that brings contentment. Create your own space that will be beneficial to your needs. Having a secret place is crucial during the process of mental transformation; this is a key to your survival. You will need a place where you can regroup. Do not openly share where your place is located. When you find your space, begin to pray in that location. As you continue to return to that location, you will begin to feel God's presence and peace in your life. Allow your secret place to become your place of safety and your fortress as you become in tune with God.

Restoration Is Free

You may be wondering, "Can my self-esteem and self-image be restored at any age, after all I have been through?"

The answer is "yes!"

Yes, it can, and God's restoration is free of charge. I spent a great deal of time and money in therapy sessions, but God does not charge for His services to restore and transform your mental state.

When a person is restored, he or she is revived back to a state of health or vigor. I love the word "vigor." Vigor is such a vibrant word. God can vigorously restore your mental health, your mind, and most of all, your soul and spirit. People pay to have psychics predict the future, and people also bury themselves in unhealthy behaviors such as illicit drugs or alcohol, explicit sexual behaviors, and the list goes on, all in search of peace and acceptance. All God requires to begin your restoration process is that you surrender your mind and heart to Him. He does not charge an entrance fee or sell an elicit product for your temporary comfort and peace. *God is the permanent solution.* He has the capabilities to give you a new mind and a new heart. Undergoing mental transformation and restoration is an amazing experience, one I look forward to you experiencing because you deserve a lifetime of peace, self-acceptance, and love. God allows the amazing experience of mental restoration, piece by piece, and you can feel your mind being transformed. As mental restoration takes place, you will see your thought process change. You will develop a productive way of thinking which will lead to positive results and outcomes and a new approach to handling life. You will take on a new outlook on life. Your view of the world and your life will change for the better. When faced with circumstances that may send you spiraling downward, you will be able to tackle them, head on, with clarity and good judgement. As you feel your mind being transformed, you will notice that you do not automatically convert to panic mode, imagining the worst outcomes. You will trust yourself with making sound, wise choices. You will see a decrease in the frequency of second-guessing. You will no longer battle indecisiveness. You will have faith in yourself. God can refresh your mind and your spirit, daily, through His Word, prayer, and His presence in your life.

A Praise Break

Something I realized as I underwent a drastic mental transformation is that I had to learn how to praise God in all circumstances. Praise is a powerful tool to utilize during the transformation process.

You must praise Him when life is going well.

You must praise Him when life is not going so well.

You must praise Him when you are in good spirits.

You must praise Him when you are not in the best spirits.

When you feel discouraged, that is the moment to give God praise. Praising God when you are discouraged brings about a spirit of gratitude and peace in your spirit and mind. As you begin to reflect on all of the obstacles God has allowed you to overcome, you will begin to anticipate greatness for your future. In turn, you will have the desire to continuously praise God. Praising God heightens your level of faith. You see, God does not change. He is not fickle. You will never catch Him having a bad day or off His game. While praising God amidst discouragement, He begins to bring back your remembrance of all His capabilities to reverse a negative circumstance, situation, or feeling. Praising God turns your tears into a smile! God wants you to praise Him for His powerful acts and His abundant greatness.

There was a time I complained more than I offered praise. However, I learned how to praise God for the present, in advance for His work behind the scenes that had not been revealed, and for what He will do in the future.

Developing a habit of praise is important. Habits are formed by repetition. Each day, make praise breaks a priority. Praise turns your attention from your problems to the Problem Solver. Praise provides you with the ability to stand, be true to yourself, and persevere despite adversity. Sometimes, you may have to praise Him through the tears. However, if you offer praise for a continuous stretch of time, those tears will turn into a smile and a spirit of gratitude. Therefore, praise God for who you are, who you are becoming, and who you will become.

The Awesomeness of Mental Peace

Today, I can express my gratitude to God for my mental peace. Attaining unwavering peace has been a long process, yet well worth the journey. I vividly remember the days of feeling unworthy and inadequate. I eventually addressed my mental disturbances, although it took some time, and I put my mental state in check. Do not allow your mental disturbances to overtake your life. Do not allow your negative thoughts to control you. Instead, control your negative thoughts by leaning on the Lord. There will be times when you must speak to Satan, boldly and forcefully, and tell him, "Not today, Satan!"

You are a steward of your mind and the thoughts that reside in your brain.

You control what thoughts should remain and what thoughts need to be dismissed.

You are the person who serves as the gatekeeper to your mind.

You are the person in charge of what enters your mind and departs from your mouth.

Remember, death and life are in the tongue!

Take the time to evaluate what mentally disturbs you, as it relates to your self-esteem and self-image. Take note of what triggers negative thoughts. Do you have negative thoughts in the presence of certain people? Is it flashbacks in your mind of past experiences? Is it all of the negativity going on in the world? Evaluate your relationships and if they could be contributing factors to how you feel about yourself. Are you involved in a relationship that is toxic to your mental state? You have the ability, with God's assistance and guidance, to set the tone and atmosphere of your mental state. Take note of the types of environments that place you in a bad mental space, as well as environments that help you be a better person. Once those determinations are made, focus on the latter. When possible, limit your exposure to people and environments that are toxic to your well-being. Make your mental peace a priority. Put yourself first and allow God to lead, guide, instruct, and direct as you transform your thought process.

I am telling you to be selfish!

Strive toward having your best interests and well-being at heart. What makes you happy? Whatever it is, as long as it is healthy, do it! Sounds simple? Well, it is. There is nothing like experiencing mental peace and a sound mind, especially when you have experienced an unsound mind filled with erratic thoughts. Allow God to control the thoughts you have toward yourself. If God's spirit controls your thinking, a life of peace will be available. Apart from God, we can do nothing!

"For God has not given us a spirit of fear and timidity, but of power, love, and self-discipline"

(2 Timothy 1:7).

"I Am" Declarations

Use the space below to develop your own "I Am" declarations (Example – I am bold! I am intelligent! I am fearfully and wonderfully made!)

_____

_____

_____

_____

_____

_____

_____

_____

_____

_____

_____

_____

_____

_____

_____

_____

_____

_____

_____

_____

Strategy #3: You Are Beautiful!

This book is all about rebuilding your self-esteem and self-image, and while I will not ramble regarding physical beauty, your outward appearance needs to be addressed because your physicality is a component of how you view yourself. How you view your outer appearance impacts your level of self-esteem.

I love being a woman. Although we experience discomforts that men do not experience, such as menstruation and childbirth, I love being a woman and all that comes with womanhood. I love my level of femininity, too. I love to feel attractive and look attractive. My husband often states that my femininity is one of my traits he was attracted to when we met. So, I take pride in my outer appearance, not only for my husband but myself.

Dressing up in a nice blouse and skirt or dress with heels just does something to my spirit, as does my face when it is lightly made up and my hair when it is freshly done. When I am dressed to my liking, I feel confident. I feel beautiful! The truth is, your physical appearance affects how you view yourself. Your self-esteem should be tied to self-care and not tied to society's standard of beauty. Please understand that your physical appearance should be measured by how you feel that day, certainly not how anyone sees you in relation to beauty. How you look, not through the eyes of someone else, plays an important role in your level of self-esteem.

There is always something that should make you feel beautiful. You may not feel like you meet the characteristics of beauty according to the world's standards but, my sister, you are beautiful, a masterpiece created by God! Song of Solomon 4:7 states, *"You are altogether beautiful, my darling, beautiful in every way."* God created all of us to have different shapes. Some of the most common female body shapes are apple, straight or narrow, pear, and hourglass. I once heard a woman say that you may even have the shape of a two-liter bottle! If that is your shape, you are beautiful, too! God created women in different sizes and shades. Whatever the case may be, God created you, and you are beautiful in His eyes. Even though you may not feel that your physical appearance is up to par, simple actions like getting a facial or a new hairstyle can make a difference in how you feel. Think about what would make you feel beautiful, and go for it! You will never know how the change will affect you if you do not try!

Physical Transformation

Despite my husband's compliments and kind words, I struggled with my appearance, yet I took action to build my confidence. There are some areas I was not pleased with, physically, so I made changes within my control. You can do the same, too.

During my teenage years, I battled with acne, and this issue carried into adulthood. I remember feeling embarrassed by severe acne flare-ups, trying to hide behind makeup. My acne flare-ups ranged from mild to severe. For many years, I was self-conscious about my skin. To this day, skin care remains important in my life. My skin reached a point when I could no longer manage this issue with over-the-counter products, leaving me no choice but to address my problem professionally. I found a dermatologist who developed the perfect treatment plan for my skin. Today, I continue to see my dermatologist, as needed, and I follow the treatment regimen she prescribed. You may think acne is no big deal, but acne was a point of concern for me, directly affecting my self-esteem. Attaining clear skin mattered to me, so I did something to change my condition.

***

I am too skinny.

I am too fat.

My hips are too wide.

My hair is too short.

My nose is too big.

We have all made negative statements, along those lines, at some point in our lives. Some women will take drastic measures, such as plastic surgery, to create change as an attempt to have what they consider the perfect body. Eating disorders derive from body image issues. Wanting to improve your appearance is perfectly fine, but make sure to exercise self-love, ensuring you are improving your appearance in a healthy manner. I encourage you to research ways to improve your physical appearance. Avoid making drastic or irreversible changes to your body or appearance. Do not make decisions regarding your appearance based on momentary emotions.

When I was in college, I thought I would look better with a different hair color. I spoke with my hairstylist about my idea. She strongly advised that my hair was too weak to handle that type of chemical. However, I took it upon myself to make the change. I thought, "If she won't do it, I will do it myself!" So, being a college student on a budget, I took the cheap route, made a trip to Walmart, and purchased a hair color that I thought I would like. Well, I freaked myself out when I saw the change in my hair! I had to swallow my pride and contact my hairstylist to fix my hair. Thankfully, she overlooked my ignorance and agreed to an emergency appointment. Of course, during the appointment, I received a lecture. Fortunately, she came to my rescue, and I did not lose all of the hair on my head. To this day, I am very cautious about hair color. So, again, think your idea through before you make a drastic change.

Most of my life, I have had a slender figure. Even while pregnant, most of my weight was baby weight, and I quickly dropped the extra pounds after giving birth. However, during my years of struggling with mental illness, my view towards my body changed. In 2008, my doctor tried different medications to treat my mental illness. Throughout that experimental time, I experienced weight gain. In July 2010, I gained 45 pounds. I believed I was going to continue gaining weight as long as I remained on the medication my doctor had prescribed, and I was not having that! Not only did I have to continue buying new clothes, but I was physically uncomfortable. Without discussing the issue with my doctor, I made the decision to abruptly stop taking the medication that I believed had caused such a significant spike in my weight. That decision resulted in disaster, and I quickly spiraled back into an episode of depression, resulting in an admission to a psychiatric unit. When I explained to my doctor why I stopped taking the medication, she empathized, yet made another change to my medication, a change which agreed with my body. In August 2010, while taking a sabbatical from my career as a social worker, I made the decision to work towards losing the weight I had gained, aiming to return to a healthy weight. I joined a gym and began working out. I also monitored what I ate, how much I ate, and when I ate. I was on a mission to reclaim my body and look like my old self again. With discipline and consistency, I lost the weight. Today, I have continued to maintain a comfortable weight.

My weight gain had a significant impact on my self-esteem. After my weight gain, my husband continued to profess his love and attraction for me, but I was disgusted by my appearance. Once I addressed the issue and began to see the results of hard work, I started to feel better about my appearance and how I felt, physically and mentally. Although individuals made comments about my weight gain, I did not lose weight for anyone else but myself. I did it for Lakeytha. I wanted to feel beautiful, and I wanted to look beautiful through my eyes. Taking pride in your appearance is important, not for the approval of others, but because we are God's creation and should conduct ourselves as such. I lost weight for me, and only me, and for that reason, I was successful. If you put your mind to a goal, you can accomplish anything.

Be your own cheerleader.

As women, we are usually our worst critics, but how about you become your biggest supporter! Patting yourself on the back is not only okay but necessary, especially if you are making progress toward a goal. The truth is, that may be the only praise you receive.

You should not only behave like who you were created to be, but you should look like who you were created to be, *a masterpiece*. You may not have the financial capabilities, but you can still look like a million bucks! My mother used to say, "You may not have much, but you do not have to look like it!" As I stated before, if you desire to improve yourself, physically, go for it. Begin making small changes. Try that new hairstyle you keep contemplating. Change your wardrobe. Experiment with your makeup. Again, do what will make you feel beautiful.

Team up with a girlfriend or another trusted woman who is willing to help you on your journey. Choose someone who will hold you accountable and celebrate your victories with you. Choose someone who will provide constructive criticism. You want someone who will build you up and be a support system.

When rebuilding your self-esteem and self-image, physical transformation is just as important as mental transformation. Ephesians 2:10 lets us know we are God's handiwork. As a masterpiece, consider the entire package.

Be Inspired

I shared several of my testimonies to inspire you to change what is in your control in a healthy manner. My goal is to inspire. Most of all, I want you to allow God to inspire you. Whatever you are battling, as it relates to your outer appearance and inner being, you are never alone. You may be embarrassed to share your struggles, but God knows your battles, and He is with you. Let God guide you by divine, supernatural influence. Psalm 29:11 lets you know that the Lord gives strength to His people; the Lord blesses His people with peace. If God and His Spirit inspire you, you will radiate with beauty, inside and out. He will give you a glow that no man-made product can produce.

Be inspired by knowing you are God's masterpiece, and you are fearfully and wonderfully made.

Be inspired by knowing you are beautiful in the eyes of God, despite the comments of man.

Be inspired by knowing you are created in His image.

"So God created human beings in his own image. In the image of God he created them; male and female he created them."

(Genesis 1:27)

List the physical qualities that you love about yourself.

_____

_____

_____

_____

_____

_____

_____

_____

_____

_____

_____

_____

_____

_____

_____

_____

_____

_____

_____

_____

_____

_____

Strategy #4: Living Up to the Proverbs 31 Woman

The Proverbs 31 woman is quite the woman, a woman with special qualities that should be practiced, daily, all of which will bring you closer to the Lord.

Her husband depends on her.

He will never be poor.

She does good for her husband, all of her life.

She never causes trouble.

She is always gathering wool and flax.

She enjoys making things with her hands.

She brings home food from everywhere.

She wakes up early in the morning, cooks food for her family, and gives the servants their share.

She looks at land and buys it.

She uses the money she has earned and plants a vineyard.

She is strong and able to do all of her work, late into the night, to make sure her business earns a profit.

She makes her clothes.

She always gives to the poor and helps those in need.

Her husband is a respected man in the community.

She speaks with wisdom and teaches others.

She is never lazy.

Wow! This is the description of the Proverbs 31 woman. Reading about her makes me tired!

The Proverbs 31 woman is a wife, mother, peacemaker, cook, realtor, entrepreneur, seamstress, philanthropist, and leader. God, you mean to tell me I must be all of this, as a woman?

Are you kidding me?

I cannot be her!

I am *not* her, and I do not want to be her!

The truth is, you do not have to be her, either. She is a guide to follow. God wants you to be the best you, not the best version of anyone else.

When you initially read about the Proverbs 31 woman, you may have become discouraged or depressed because this woman the Bible raves about is everything you may not be yet. You may wonder:

How can I live up to her? She is everything I am not.

She is resourceful. She is innovative. She is business savvy. She is a gourmet cook. If only I had one of her talents or traits, I would be an awesome woman.

Well, despite what you consider a lack of talents or traits, you are still a phenomenal woman!

I used to beat myself up about all the tasks I could not do and the talents and qualities I was lacking. I often compared myself to my mother, my sister, and other women who seemed to have gifts I did not possess. I felt boring and that there was not too much excitement about me. I felt inadequate due to what I perceived as lack of talents. I often felt ashamed of not having the ability or desire to do something I felt I should be doing as a woman. I was quick to ponder on what I could not do well, or even at all, as opposed to celebrating what I could do and the talents I did possess.

I am a practical woman. Place me in a room full of women, and I probably would not be the most creative.

I am not a gourmet cook. I cook because my family and I must eat to survive.

I am not athletic, unlike my sister who was a skillful athlete on the basketball team and track and field team in high school.

The list goes on, and I am okay with my imperfections because I can only be the best me. I have come to realize I am the Proverbs 31 woman in my own right, and that is perfectly fine because God created me this way. In the past, I have attempted to make myself enjoy something or be something I was not created to be as a woman. Trying to force yourself to be someone you are not in an attempt to impress people is unhealthy and detrimental. Take on tasks or roles because you enjoy those activities. Otherwise, you will feel miserable. Sometimes, you have to exit your comfort zone, but make sure you are stepping out of your comfort zone for the correct reasons. With God's help, you can create your version of the Proverbs 31 woman.

Build on Your Strengths

We have different gifts, and each gift came because of the grace God gave us (Romans 12:6). This scripture further states that whoever has the gift of serving should serve (Romans 12:7). Whoever has the gift of comforting others should do that. Whoever has the gift of giving help to others should give generously. You get the picture. Work your gifts and talents! *Seek God to enlarge your territory as it relates to utilizing your gifts and talents.* God made you who you are so that you would spend your life doing the good things he has planned for you (Ephesians 2:10).

When you read about the Proverbs 31 woman, she seems like an incredibly talented woman who has life together. In my opinion, she is a bit intimidating! She appears to be extremely skillful, and she has excellent time management skills! She seems extraordinary, but so are you! There is nothing common or ordinary about you! We have different levels and degrees of abilities and strengths. Offer your abilities and strengths to God, and make yourself available for His use. Allow God to use you so that you may help someone else. No one can take your abilities and strengths from you. They are your possessions, and they have been copyrighted by God! Treasure your abilities and strengths. Your abilities, strengths, talents, and gifts will make room for you in this great big world. The scripture lets you know that your gifts can open many doors and help you meet other important people (Proverbs 18:16). He can and will help you maximize your strengths.

We all have weaknesses and shortcomings. However, do not focus on what you cannot do or your lack of knowledge. Do not allow your focus on your weaknesses and shortcomings to consume you. Focusing on weaknesses and shortcomings can become a stumbling block in your growth. In fact, Satan will play on your fixation, causing you to focus on what you cannot do or be and make those shortcomings seem more important. Praise God for your resourcefulness, creativity, gifts, and talents. Consider those qualities priceless as you evolve into the woman God created.

You are unique and original!

Celebrate your authenticity!

A Faithful Woman

There is no denying that God is always faithful. In His Word, you can find numerous scriptures of His faithfulness. Psalm 33:4 states, *"For the word of the Lord holds true, and we can trust everything he does."* In 2 Timothy 2:13, the verse reads, *"If we are unfaithful, he remains faithful, for he cannot deny who he is."* He has been, continues to be, and will always be true to His Word. I encourage you to be faithful and committed to what you are called to do as it relates to your strengths, talents, gifts, and abilities. Remain steady in your allegiance, not only to people but God, most importantly. Your faithfulness with all He has entrusted you with will result in blessings.

There are many accounts of different faithful women in the Bible: Hannah, Abigail, Ruth, and Naomi, to name a few. If you study their stories, you will notice they were all faithful to what they were called to do during a season in their life. Hannah is one of my favorite biblical women. Hannah was unable to conceive for a long time, and she was provoked and taunted by her husband's second wife who had been able to birth children. Hannah did not respond vengefully, but she poured out her heart and sorrow to God, allowing Him to vindicate her. Eventually, Hannah's faithful prayer life and outpour of her heart to God paid off. She conceived, and she was able to give her husband a son, Samuel.

Remaining faithful to your gifts and talents will take you places you may never have imagined. I am a witness. Several characteristics accompany faithfulness:

Devotion.

Support.

Loyalty.

Consistency.

Perseverance.

Apply these characteristics to the strengths, gifts, and talents for which God has blessed you.

A Woman of Vision

As little girls, some of us dreamed of what we wanted to be when we grew up. My daughter talks about what she wants to be when she grows up, too. I came to realize it is important to teach her to prepare for *who* she wants to be when she grows up. As adults, we must examine the same line of questions:

Who are you now?

Who do you want to be in the future?

Who has God called you to be?"

In high school, I wanted to be a nurse, mostly because my mother is a nurse. God blessed me with the motivation to graduate and enroll in college, majoring in nursing. I studied nursing for the first two years of college, completing a semester of clinical work as a student nurse. After beginning my clinical, I realized that the nursing profession was not for me, but I struggled with fear, fear of disappointing the people who were rooting for me. Nevertheless, at the age of 20, I knew that nursing was not His vision for my life. I came to terms with this realization and changed my major to social work, allowing me to remain in the helping-hands industry. Today, I am a Licensed Master Social Worker in the state of Louisiana. I love my profession, and I am grateful that I decided to change my major. I encourage you always to follow your heart. Being a social worker, a wife, and a mother are roles and components of my life, but those roles are not solely who I am in life.

I have a vision of who I want to be as I continue this journey called life. I am a wife, a mother, a daughter, a sister, and a friend, but first, I am a woman of God. I have a vision of what I want to see occur and what I want to experience in this lifetime. My priorities are my husband and my children, but I will not use them as obstacles to being a woman of vision. There is nothing wrong with desiring to be the best wife and mother because those are outstanding roles. Speak for yourself. Declare and decree the goals you would like to see come to pass in your life. Publishing a book was a component of my vision, and here I am! I am a published author! I am proud and humbled by what God has allowed me to accomplish.

Scripture instructs writing down what the Lord reveals. Write the words clearly so the message will be easy to read. The message is about a special time in the future, and it will come true. Be patient, and wait. The time will not be late (Habakkuk 2:2-3). Write your vision! I wrote my vision and presented it to God for His approval and assistance. As a Proverbs 31 woman, present your vision to God. If you remain in the Will of God, He will bring your vision to pass. Do not focus on what you may be lacking. If you have God on your side, that is what and who you need to persevere. Trust God with your vision and allow Him to place His stamp of approval on your goal. With God on your side, your opportunities are limitless. Release your potential, and follow your vision!

A Woman of Great Influence

When I think of the word *influence,* power, authority, leadership, prestige, and significance are words that come to mind. At some point in life, you influence others in some form. Good or bad, you have the capabilities to influence someone else.

As a mother, I learned that I have significant influence over my daughter. I can recall her stating, as a little girl, that she wanted to be a mommy when she grows up. At the age of 13, I continue to have significant influence over her, and she is constantly listening to what I am saying, watching how I carry myself, and keeping an eye on my actions and, might I add, she has no problem asking questions if she is puzzled by something I do or say. My daughter motivates me to be a better wife, mother, and woman because I am the first example she sees of a woman. My goal is to set the best possible example. I realized, a long time ago, that I play a major role in how she will develop as she transitions into womanhood. Therefore, knowing I am a woman of influence, not only in my daughter's life but in the lives of other young ladies and women whom I mentor, I make sure that I am leading the best possible example.

Never underestimate the impact of your presence and influence in someone's life. People may not frequently or openly verbalize how you are impacting their lives, but in time, it will be revealed. You never know how your words or actions can change the perspective and outlook of another life. My blog and this book are dear to my heart because these are avenues which provide me with a platform to share God's goodness. Everyone may not be interested in hearing or reading what you have to say, but when the opportunity presents itself for you to share with someone, and they are eager to listen, you should share.

Women deal with so much in life because of the many roles we fulfill. Therefore, it is imperative for us to share some of our struggles and obstacles as well as our triumphs and victories with each other. Remind one another that there is always hope! You never know whose life you will influence and how God will use you to bless another person.

The Key to Success

The Proverbs 31 woman appears to be the entire package. She appears to have the ability to do everything and anything, for anyone, at any time. The portrait painted of her is that of an amazing woman. As you read about her, you may wonder who in the world has the time and energy to do what she does, especially if you work outside of the home. The Proverbs 31 woman has five noticeable traits:

She can be trusted.

She is consistent.

She is strong.

She is a go-getter.

She is wise.

So, how is she able to be so successful?

The key to her success is that she fears the Lord. She has an unwavering reverence for Him. Because she fears the Lord, she is a beautiful person with a beautiful life. She places God *first*, not her husband, her children, or her business, but God!

Fearing God entails having the deepest respect for Him and the power He holds. Fearing God is not about His wrath because He does everything out of love. Fearing God is about knowing the extraordinary things He can and will do in your life. The Proverbs 31 woman was most likely an ordinary woman, like you and I, but when she placed God first, He turned her from an ordinary woman into an extraordinary woman.

I encourage you to allow God to lead and direct your steps. Follow His instructions. The result of that formula is *success!* There is no other woman more beautiful in the eyes of God than a virtuous, God-fearing woman. If you bestow honor upon God, you can live up to the expectations of the Proverbs 31 woman.

"Charm is deceptive, and beauty does not last; but a woman who fears the Lord will be greatly praised"

(Proverbs 31:30).

Create a plan for yourself, outlining your goals and the vision you have for your life for the next six months. Then, create another plan for your goals and vision for the next year and the next five years.

_____

_____

_____

_____

_____

_____

_____

_____

_____

_____

_____

_____

_____

_____

_____

_____

_____

_____

_____

_____

_____

_____

_____

_____

_____

_____

_____

_____

_____

_____

_____

_____

_____

_____

_____

_____

_____

_____

_____

_____

_____

_____

_____

_____

Strategy #5: The Least Can Be the Greatest

Are you not where you thought you would be at this stage of your life?

Do you feel as though you do not have what it takes to see your vision or goals come to life?

I can relate to those doubts because I have been there. Due to my struggles with mental illness, it took me a long time to realize that I was capable of being successful as a wife, mother, woman in ministry, career woman, and so forth. My history of mental illness birthed the thought that I would never be "good enough" to do anything worthwhile or do anything well. My history of mental illness caused me to fear doing anything new or different because I felt as though I never knew when I would have another episode. The shame of experiencing mental illness overshadowed the idea that I could be great at anything.

When you are chosen by God, your family circumstances, socioeconomic status, and education level do not matter. When you are chosen by God, your past does not matter, either. God can and will use anyone He chooses. Joshua 2 is about a prostitute, Rahab, who hid two spies in her home. She placed her life on the line for two men she did not know. Rahab's cooperation to assist the spies in reaching their goal was the major factor for the spies fulfilling their assignment. The Israelites were able to arrive to the Promised Land.

Because of her role, she is listed in the Hall of Fame for faith in Hebrews 11. Can you imagine how she must have felt as a prostitute? The ridicule she must have faced, and the shame she must have experienced, was probably unbearable. Despite her background, God used her. I can imagine Rahab had an appreciation for herself and her life after those life-changing events. I can imagine Rahab looking in the mirror, thinking, "Did I really assist two men who served God? Me? A prostitute? Really?" I'm sure that accomplishment allowed a significant change for her, mentally and spiritually. I imagine her view of herself made a 180-degree change.

Despite your past, God loves you, and He can use you for His glory! Build on your strengths. You may be struggling with your past or present experiences, but know that you are valuable and you can be utilized to perform tremendous tasks. As a result of my history of mental illness, I consider myself a qualified spokesperson for mental illness, particularly, depression. My "mess" was turned into a message and my "test" into a testimony! Recognize your value and worth as a woman. I never thought I would be strong enough to share some of my struggles with the world, but here I am, boldly sharing my experiences. I was not sure I had what it takes to become a published author, but here I am! I had no idea where to begin nor did I have any idea as to how I would have to the time to write with my hectic lifestyle, connect to the right people, and have the resources to fulfill my dream of writing and publishing a book. To sum it up, God provided the perfect timing, resources, and the right connections! He receives *all* the recognition for *Loving God's Masterpiece.*

Where you have come from has no bearing on where you are going. No one is a match for God. God will equip you to perform the tasks He called you to do.

If God says, "Yes, it is time to begin walking in your purpose," then begin moving forward.

If God opens a door of opportunity, prepare to walk through that door.

Never allow anyone to make you feel insignificant or inferior. Be confident in who you are and whom you belong. Do not allow your past or present to create the idea that you have not or will not amount to anything in life. That thought process is a tactic of Satan. People may place a negative label on you, but do not accept the label. You may even have to remove the label you have placed on yourself. If you are labeled negatively, avoid living up to that label and demonstrate who you are in Christ and what He can do through you. The only label relevant to your life is the one God places on you.

Speak over your life.

Condition your mind to be the greatest through God, and He will strengthen you. *Develop a spirit of excellence, not mediocrity.* Everyone's level of excellence will not look identical. Embrace your purpose. If you are not sure what your purpose is at this point, seek the One who has the answer. Ephesians 1:11 informs us that we are chosen to be God's people in Christ, and He makes everything agree with what He decides and wants. If you are having a difficult time finding your purpose or understanding your purpose, pray using these words:

Dear God, I know there is a great purpose for me while on Earth. I do not know where to begin regarding my purpose. I ask that you help me find my way. I ask that each morning I rise, you guide me through my day, opening doors of opportunities to help me discover who I am. I ask these things in Jesus name.

Remain in Position

Becoming consumed and overwhelmed by difficult circumstances is seemingly easy. Sometimes, seeing the light at the end of the tunnel is difficult. You may be in a place you had not imagined or anticipated but remain in position to be blessed by God. Shift your focus to the place where you envision yourself in the future. Set your eyes on the prize. *Stand up, stand firm, and stand out!* There may be individuals who are counting you out. In fact, you may be counting yourself out, but you must learn to take your eyes off of your circumstances and place your eyes on God. You have to see beyond the present. Keep Hebrews 11:1 at the forefront of your mind: *"Faith shows the reality of what we hope for; it is the evidence of things we cannot see."*

Live your life in expectation of all God is going to bless you with and what a success you will be if you remain loyal to Him. Remain in position to be blessed. We all have battles, some of which are publicly known and some of which only you and God know. Succumbing to feelings of defeat, if you do not see the desired results at a rapid rate, is easy. It is also easy to become overwhelmed by obstacles, but convert those obstacles into stepping stones to becoming a better you. Transformation will require you to pace yourself and be comfortable with where you are positioned while you are moving towards your desires. You have to remain in position despite the pressures you may experience. Prepare to receive all the blessings God has for you. Remember, success usually does not happen overnight. Regardless of your problems, public or private, you are a precious jewel in the eyes of God: *"But you belong to God, my dear children. You have already won a victory over those people, because the Spirit who lives in you is great than the spirit who lives in the world"* (1 John 4:4).

God has hidden many blessings for you. You will receive them in due time if you live your life in expectation of receiving those blessings. Trust Him and His timing, and He will bless you, so all the world may see His glory!

Your Journey

Follow and appreciate your journey.

Life often brings unexpected twists and turns, and life may not go as planned. In fact, life will not go as planned. As you read this book, you may be questioning how you reached your current state. Well, at this point, the focus should not be solely on how you got where you are, but where you are going. God is the giver of life, and He is the sustainer of your life despite how you may feel about your life. You can be clueless as to where God is going to lead you, but cluelessness does not permit you to step off the course God has paved. Have you ever thought to yourself, "I didn't see that coming!" Well, that unexpected move was God! If you allow Him to order your steps, the journey will be much smoother to follow and accept, along with all the events that accompany it, whether trying, favorable, pleasant, or difficult. Psalm 37:23 states, *"The Lord directs the steps of the godly. He delights in every detail of their lives."*

When you resist God, you are asking for trouble. God does not force you to do anything, but He is not obligated to bless your plans if He does not approve.

Be mindful that your journey is not supposed to be a replica of another woman's journey. You are not supposed to have the same circumstances, outcomes, or results because your journey is unique. You are unique. Your journey has not been cloned and will not be cloned. Out of the billions of people in this world, your journey is undoubtedly unique. Take pride and comfort in knowing that God positioned you for unique circumstances. We each have our own story. In one of my husband's sermons, he stated, "Life comes down to making decisions. God is waiting for you to decide to hear Him, to believe Him, and to obey Him." Make the decision that you will live life to the fullest and make the most of each day.

Always look for life lessons as you encounter different experiences. I have often asked God, "What are you trying to show me in this situation?" In November 2017, I was informed that my position with a reputable health insurance company was being eliminated due to workforce reductions. I had never experienced a layoff or termination; therefore, this was a hard pill to swallow. I thought I had an amazing job with an excellent salary and great benefits. I wondered why God would take that from me. After the initial shock and disappointment dwindled, I began to seek God to receive revelation regarding the lesson to be taken away from this experience, and He provided revelation! Today, I have accepted that He closed that chapter of my life for a purpose, to begin my next chapter in life as a published author. This book was birthed once he closed that chapter of my life!

Success does not come without costs. Anything you want to achieve requires work and discipline, including your level of self-love, but first and foremost, your success requires your acknowledgment of God as director of your life. God wants you to thrive on your journey, but it is up to you how you will embrace your journey. Walk your journey with honor, purpose, and courage!

Plan for Success

At the start of a new year, I do not make resolutions. Instead, I set goals. I write my goals so I can refer to them to monitor my progress. To be successful in achieving my goals, I know I must put forth the effort, commitment, discipline, and determination, in addition to conditioning my mind for success. Success is a mindset. Whether you speak positive or negative affirmations is a major factor in your success.

An example of a positive affirmation would be, "I got this! I am moving into bigger and better things!"

An example of a negative affirmation would be, "I will never get this done! I am so tired of dealing with this! This will never work!"

I encourage you to avoid the latter. Negative affirmations will never result in success. If you expect success, you will have a higher percentage of being successful. If you expect to fail, you will have a higher percentage of failing. We often receive what we expect! I have learned to prepare for success. I envision myself being victorious. I envision that goal coming to fruition. You must place your mind in the proper state to be successful. Success is a process. It does not occur overnight. It will take some time to undo your negative pattern of thinking. Achieving your goals may be difficult at first, especially if you are used to entertaining the mindset of failure and defeat. Being successful requires a mindset of victory. The more you engage as it relates to success, your mind will begin to reprogram, only entertaining thoughts of success. Planning for success requires repetition and encouragement. Developing a habit, good or bad, usually takes 21 days. However, it may require a little more time when conditioning your mind for success, and that is okay. Developing a habit took me longer than 21 days!

Take one day at a time.

Take one goal at a time.

Take one circumstance at a time.

A strength of mine is multi-tasking, but some may not have this as their strong suit, and that is okay. Some tasks require attention and time. Move at a pace which will work for you and guarantee that you stick to working towards your goals. Be comfortable with following your timetable, but more importantly, God's timetable. I know we sometimes do not like God's timetable because God sees time differently from us, but if you follow it, you are guaranteed the best possible outcome. Again, trust God's timing and His process. Allow God to put His agenda into effect. Let nothing or no one serve as an obstacle or distraction as you go before God and the throne of grace with your goals and desires.

Be determined to be successful in everything you pursue. If one door closes, understand that God has permitted that door to close in preparation for better doors to open. If God closes the door, let it go and move on! Trying to reopen a door closed by God is a waste of time and effort because it simply is not possible. *The steps of a good woman are ordered by the Lord.* Therefore, make sure He is ordering your steps!

"That is what the Scriptures mean when they say, 'No eye has seen, no ear has heard, and no mind has imagined what God has prepared for those who love him."

(I Corinthians 2:9)

List the successes you have accomplished in your life, emotionally, spiritually, and professionally.

_____

_____

_____

_____

_____

_____

_____

_____

_____

_____

_____

_____

_____

_____

_____

_____

_____

_____

_____

_____

_____

_____

Strategy #6: Living as a New Creature

On May 4, 1999, I accepted Christ into my life and was filled with His Holy Spirit on August 20, 1999. I was tired of making poor decisions, and I desired a sense of peace in my life. The time had come to acknowledge Christ and develop a relationship with Him. At that point, I was officially "a new creature" according to God's Word. I had a new identity. I had a new walk and a new talk. I even had a new way of dressing. I can vividly remember having a burning fire and passion regarding my new life in Christ. However, after becoming a wife and mother, maintaining that fire was a struggle. Life began to happen, sometimes causing the fire to not burn as aggressively as it once did. I did not only experience being on a mental and emotional roller coaster, but I experienced being on a spiritual roller coaster, too. The mental, emotional, and spiritual roller coaster was not a ride of thrills. It was scary. I was uncertain how I would wake up feeling from day to day. I could begin the day feeling hopeful, and by the time nightfall came, I could be wishing I was dead.

Struggling with guilt, inadequacy, and hypocrisy as a born-again believer was draining. In some instances, I experienced feelings that I was a vessel for God's use, openly expressing my gratitude, proclaiming to have an unshakeable faith and remembering that God is my Source, only to return to thoughts of suicide, shame, and torment. Feelings of numbness and emptiness consumed my heart and soul, which was an exhausting manner of living. I have shed so many tears. Feeling as though I was continuously under Satan's attack was tough to endure. I was experiencing this battle, all while declaring myself a believer. At one point, I can recall questioning if God's Holy Spirit continued to dwell inside of me. He seemed so far away.

Through the heartache, the doubt, and the tears, God restored me as a believer and continuously revived my soul. God allowed me to undergo a mental transformation in February 2014, but He also allowed me to experience a spiritual transformation, too. God began to release me from the mental and spiritual bondage that bound me for so many years. I began to see and appreciate the extraordinary life God blessed me to have. Yes, you read it correctly! I said, "extraordinary", because life is so precious. That is a term now in my vocabulary as a result of recognizing I am a *masterpiece*. He began to bring me back to life as "a new creature." He changed me, once again, allowing me to recognize that I must focus on spiritual growth. Once I placed spiritual growth as priority, all other aspects of my life began to fall in line and change for the better. He gave me a new passion for Him, my relationship with Him, and His Word. He gave me a new passion for life, my life! He gifted me with the desire to communicate with Him through prayer on a consistent basis.

God helped me to alter a mind of worry and anxiety into a mind of trust and peace. My many nights of insomnia turned into peaceful nights of rest. I renewed my commitment to spending time with God, desiring all He had for my life. I rededicated my life, my mind, my spirit, and my body to God. I rededicated myself to being the God-fearing woman I knew He called me to be. He guided me in realizing and accepting I was His masterpiece. God called to my attention that I was a walking miracle. In His eyes, I am splendid, remarkable, marvelous, incomparable, and a treasure! If he cleared my low-grade vision of myself, He could do the same for you. God can transform you into "a new creature." He can heal you and redeem you. He can restore you and return what you feel you lost. In fact, he can provide you with better than what you previously lost. He can give a double portion as described in the story of Job in the Bible.

Restoration and redemption begin when you surrender your entire being to God and allow yourself to be vulnerable. We are usually careful with who we let our guard down with or who we allow to see our vulnerability, but there is no need to be that way with God. He is your Creator, and He knows your innermost struggles and pain.

Restoration and redemption begin when you acknowledge that you are broken in spirit and have wounds that need to be healed.

Restoration and redemption begin once you forgive yourself for any form of self-sabotage.

Restoration and redemption begin when you are ready to move forward with your purpose.

Another Chance

Each morning, you are blessed to open your eyes, and you are blessed to have another chance to improve. God is not a God of second chances, but He is a God of another chance. Man will quickly turn his back on you if he feels you do not meet his standards, but God does not operate in that manner. God's Word says His mercy is new, every morning, not once a week, once a month, or once a year, but every morning (Lamentations 3:23). Praise God for His grace and mercy. Where would we be without those two gifts? I know I would not be in this wonderful place without His everlasting mercy.

There will be moments when you will have a struggle that you cannot seem to shake. You will have personal struggles that require several attempts to overcome. Dealing with strongholds is no joking matter. I must warn you – from time to time, you may feel frustrated by slow progress, or what appears to be lack of progress, during your transformation, but do not stop moving forward! You will have days when you are not sure you are traveling in the right direction but stay on course.

What you must recognize is that your issues regarding self-esteem did not occur overnight; those issues were a gradual process. Therefore, be patient. Be patient with yourself because God is patient with you. During your transformation, you may wake up with a mind filled with negativity, but go to your secret place and tell God about your thoughts. You may even shed tears, but those tears eventually turn into a smile. A good cry is therapeutic! Remember, He will turn those tears into a smile and weakness into strength.

Do not become discouraged if you do not see immediate changes. Let God work in you, and praise Him for giving you another chance. Do not entertain thoughts contrary to God and His Word. Experiencing thoughts of discouragement is a tactic of Satan. Satan knows that discouragement will result in stagnancy. Do not give him that satisfaction or the power. Dismiss him, immediately, when you consider giving up. Never give up on your vision. Never give up on being successful. Remember who you are in the eyes of God... *a masterpiece!*

God continues to give me the nudge I need to move forward. I continuously pray without ceasing, and I work toward my goals. Prayer is the key to living and maintaining as a new creature. There is nothing you cannot share with God. I promise you, He will not judge you; He will give you another chance, and another chance, and another chance! Every morning, I wake up and view the day as a new opportunity to make progress with my vision and my goals. There are several areas of my life where I have made momentous progress which gives me hope that there are more positive changes to come. I love my life and all God created me to be! Sometimes, all you need to see is a glimpse of light at the end of the tunnel, and it serves as motivation to press forward. You must learn to celebrate small victories; it does not matter what anyone else may think. If it is important to you, celebrate. There may be times when only you and God will celebrate, and that is okay! You want Him to celebrate with you. He is all the applause you will ever need. Utilize every new opportunity that God gives you to produce a new, improved you. Avoid seeing yourself as complex or complicated. Remember, you are unique! You can be changed and re-invented. Ask God to guide you in recognizing distinct opportunities to improve yourself.

A New Existence

But forget all that – it is nothing compared to what I am going to do. For I am about to do something new. See, I have already begun! Do you not see it? I will make a pathway through the wilderness. I will create rivers in the dry wasteland.

Those are the words written in Isaiah 43:18-19. As a new creature, these words must be embedded in your mind as you allow God to transform your life.

When someone reminds you of your past, remember that God is doing a "new thing" with you.

When you want to beat yourself up for past mistakes, remember that God is doing a "new thing" with you.

When the enemy wants to plant thoughts of shame and guilt, remember that God is doing a "new thing" with you.

When you feel as though you have not amounted to anything, remember that God is doing a "new thing" with you.

When you feel discouraged about your progress, remember that God is doing a "new thing" with you.

Remind yourself that you *are* a "new thing!"

There have been occasions when I felt disturbed by something from my past, a particular stronghold. For a long time, the fear of battling a mental illness again was constantly reappearing. When I would think about that stronghold, a sense of nervousness would arise. I would wonder how long the streak of having good days would last. Satan would begin to taunt me regarding the stronghold; however, the Holy Spirit would quickly remind me that God does not go back on His promises once He delivers you. I simply had to take one day at a time and celebrate each passing day that I remained free. The Holy Spirit reminds me that I have been delivered and set free. As a new creature, Satan does not want to see you flourish, and he will do anything to cause regression. He will use people, he will use circumstances, and he will even use you against yourself.

In certain instances, reflecting on the past is acceptable and spiritually healthy, mainly when remembering how God delivered you out of a situation or mindset. Now, when I reflect on my lengthy past of mental illness, I can smile and shed tears of gratitude to see the amazing progress I have made in the past eight years. However, to dwell on past mistakes and shortcomings, focusing on the negative components of those events, is not mentally or spiritually healthy. Releasing the past is the tool that allows you to embrace your present and look forward to your future. Even the events of yesterday are considered the past. Do not continually replay past negative experiences or conversations in your mind. It is impossible to change the past; therefore, it does not benefit you to relive those moments constantly. Replace the memories of the past with visions of the bright future that is headed your way. Envision yourself as the woman you desire to be and are working to become. I encourage you to create a visual in your mind of the woman you are striving to become. Visualize yourself doing big things!

Continuously ponder on the bright future that is ahead.

Continuously ponder on the progress you have made and continue to make.

Continuously ponder on all the great changes that are taking place in your life.

Continuously ponder on how God has delivered you, and is delivering you, from dark places in your life.

Remember, today is a new day with new opportunities. Today is a day of another chance. Today is a new day with a new thing, you, God's *masterpiece*! Praise God for a new thing.

Live for today!

Enjoy today!

Embrace today!

Celebrate today!

Be happy today!

Keep in mind, you are the only one who controls your thoughts, emotions, words, and actions. Those responsibilities belong to you and no one else. Hold yourself accountable. Choose to enjoy this day and bless the name of the Lord despite what may or may not occur and how you may feel. I am constantly reminding myself that this is the day the Lord has made, especially on those mornings when I am just not "feeling" it!

I consistently think of the awesomeness of God and my many blessings to maintain a positive attitude. I realize the importance of staying in tune with God, filling my life with His presence, His Word, and His joy.

The Mind of Christ

A mindset is your way of thinking, your thought process. Everything you do in life begins with your thoughts. Your thoughts are the root of everything you say and how you behave. As God began to transform me, mentally and spiritually, it was imperative that I remembered to maintain my mind in the proper condition to handle my responsibilities. Satan's mindsets are those in which are filled with doubt, insecurity, confusion, and anxiety. I can testify to having experienced all of those conditions of the mind, resulting in my inability to accomplishing anything with ease. Make life easier for yourself. Choose to walk in joy, light, positivity, and assurance, and when you find yourself taking two steps back, choose to seek His light. When you seek Him, and all His glory, you will find yourself on the right path, completely drifting away from Satan's plans.

When you possess the mind of Christ, you can think positive thoughts. Having the mind of Christ allows your thoughts to be on God and His mighty works. When your thoughts are erratic and distorted, remembering that God loves you is a challenge. You will not be able to function in that manner. Paul the Apostle instructs you to hold your thoughts captive and make them obedient to Christ. The mind is a terrible thing to waste, right? That statement is true, but more importantly, having a sound mind is truly a gift from God.

Treasure the gift. A sound mind is a vital link in living how God intended you to live your earthly life. It is critical that you nourish your mind, daily. What you feed your mind will eventually come out in your speech and actions. Proper nourishment will empower you to consistently be aware that you are a precious commodity to God.

Preservation

There are multiple meanings of the word "preserve." Preserve means to keep alive, to protect, or to spare. As a woman of God, I know God preserves me, day to day. I also act to aide in my preservation. I pray, daily. I study God's Word. I read books and watch programs that will keep me in the right frame of mind. I remain in the company of the right type of people. I laugh. I remain positive. I enjoy life. I make sure I do all I know how to do to move in the right direction. It was Him who preserved me amid mental turmoil. When I do not receive eight hours of sleep every night or eat three healthy meals each day, He maintains my physical existence. Just as He maintains my physical existence, he maintains my spiritual existence, too. I am aware that He preserves me during trouble. Despite life's circumstances, God is consistent in preserving your life. The world is constantly changing, but scripture lets us know that Jesus is the same yesterday, today, and forevermore (Hebrews 13:8).

If He kept you yesterday, He can keep you today, and He will keep you tomorrow. I find tremendous comfort in knowing that God does not have any hidden agendas or secret motives. I am free to be myself with Him. He loves me as I am. I have been accused of having a touch of Obsessive Compulsive Disorder (by my loving daughter), which does have some truth to it! I have always liked structure. I am a creature of habit, and I like routine. I know God loves me and will preserve me, OCD personality and all! He has the capabilities to preserve your mind during mental chaos, disorders, and disturbances. He will preserve you as a "new creature."

Maintenance of a New Creature

As God transforms you, it is critical to maintain your self-esteem and self-image. As God began to transform my life, I truly began to love who I was becoming. Today, I continue to love the woman I have become and I look forward to seeing what God will continue to do for my life and where He is going to take me. I treasure myself. I appreciate feelings of peace and happiness. Therefore, I have no desire to return to the dark place God had delivered me from. Today, I am constantly praying and feeding my mind with God's Word to nurture my self-esteem. Two of my favorite scriptures that I think of on a daily basis are Jeremiah 29:11 (*"'For I know the plans I have for you', says the Lord. 'They are plans for good and not for disaster, to give you a future and a hope.'"*) and Ephesians 3:20 (*"Now all glory to God, who is able, through his mighty power at work within us, to accomplish infinitely more than we might ask or think."*)

In maintaining yourself, you must deliberately talk to yourself, daily. Yes, talk to yourself! Self-talk is vital in cultivating self-confidence. You must verbalize your "I AM" factors, daily. It is imperative to remind yourself that, "I AM beautiful", "I AM smart", "I AM a strong woman", and, of course, "I AM a masterpiece!"

Surround yourself with supportive and positive people. Avoid negative individuals. Those people will only serve as a hindrance and distraction to your growth. Maintenance may require you to sever toxic relationships. Toxic relationships involve individuals with bad attitudes, individuals who are constantly complaining, individuals who find fault in others, individuals who discourage your growth, individuals who have jealous and envious spirits, individuals who are always telling you why "this or that" will never work, and individuals who are bitter and angry. Surrounding yourself with toxic people and relationships will result in stagnancy or regression. *Some people were intended to be in your life for a season or not at all.* Do not fret if you lose relationships because God will replace those relationships with individuals who love and appreciate you. Pray for relationships that will bring out the best in you. Pray that God will place the right people in your life at the right time. Continue to increase your feelings of worth and value. Continue to strive in going higher and higher. There should be no looking back, only pressing forward.

True Joy and Contentment

The late Billy Graham stated:

Joy cannot be pursued. It comes from within. It is a state of being. It does not depend on circumstances, but triumphs over circumstances. It produces a gentleness of spirit and a magnetic personality.

Kay Warren, co-founder of Saddleback Church, describes joy as the settled assurance that God is in control of the details of your life, the quiet confidence that everything will be alright, and the determined choice to praise God in every situation. In her description, three keywords stood out: *assurance, confidence,* and *determination.*

Be assured that God can give you true joy and contentment. Be determined to live a life filled with joy and contentment. Your confidence should result from the reflection of your previous experiences with God. Your determination should be driven by the desire to continue living as a new creature in Christ.

Joy does not come naturally, and it does not stem from external factors such as income, lifestyle, or health. A person can have a six-figure income and not experience joy. Joy derives from internal factors such as faith and hope. Joy includes contentment, too. You can maintain joy when you become content with how God created you.

Contentment is a state of satisfaction. Contentment does not mean you do not desire more for yourself; contentment is a state of appreciation for where you are now. I live by a scripture by Paul the Apostle. In Philippians 4:11, Paul states, *"Not that I was ever in need, for I have learned how to be content with whatever I have."*

When you feel the urge to become frustrated and complain, remind yourself of that scripture. When suffering from self-esteem and self-image issues, it may take some time to reach a state of joy regarding your life and feeling content with your present state; therefore, be patient with yourself. Developing a state of joy and contentment will require reprogramming your mind.

Does maintaining joy and contentment require constant effort?

Yes, but exhibiting a state of perpetual joy is entirely possible!

Will you occasionally shed tears while trying to maintain your joy?

Yes, as I shared earlier, you will. However, those tears will only be temporary because God will permanently comfort you!

"This means that anyone who belongs to Christ has become a new person. The old life is gone; a new life has begun!"

(II Corinthians 5:17)

List the positive changes that have occurred in your life.

_____

_____

_____

_____

_____

_____

_____

_____

_____

_____

_____

_____

_____

_____

_____

_____

_____

_____

_____

_____

_____

_____

Strategy #6: Living as a New Creature

_____

_____

_____

_____

_____

_____

_____

_____

_____

_____

_____

_____

_____

_____

_____

_____

_____

_____

_____

_____

_____

_____

_____

_____

_____

Strategy #7: Moving Forward

Women are stereotypically more inclined to hold on to anger, resentment, and bitterness regarding painful past experiences. If we are not careful, we will continue to relive painful experiences or mistakes from years ago, as if those situations happened yesterday. However, you cannot move forward while holding on to the past. I know what it's like to deal with regret, shame, guilt, and disappointment. I know what it's like to deal with pain from the past and not see a bright future because of a stronghold on what occurred yesterday, last month, last year, or several years ago. I have also experienced God taking the pain of the past and turning that pain into hope for the future, giving me the desire to move forward.

God allowed me to become tired of carrying the weight and burdens I placed upon myself. He showed me I would not be able to move forward while holding on to my past. One of the problems I had that contributed to my mental illness was that I had not let go of the resentment and anger I harbored towards my biological father and the loving father-daughter relationship he deprived me of as a child and as an adult. For years, I buried my feelings. I thought I was okay until an encounter or conversation with my father caused those feelings to resurface. I had to deal with my unresolved issues, and I came to realize that I could not change the past, but I do have control of my behavior and my future. Sometimes, we become stuck in a place, unable to identify the cause. I encourage you to do a self-inventory to locate any feelings or experiences that may be holding you back from moving forward. Self-inventory consists of taking note of the thoughts that are playing in your mind as well as your behavior and reactions to daily situations and circumstances. When you notice a negative reaction to a situation, immediately ask yourself, "Why do I feel this way" or "what is making me behave this way?" Sometimes, the answer will be simple. For instance, your response may be due to fatigue or exhaustion. Other times, the answer may not be that simple and you will have to dig a little deeper. Collecting self-inventory may require you to face deep issues, head on, but collecting self-inventory is imperative if you desire to move forward as the woman God created you to be. As you move forward as a new creature, God will continue to restore you. Psalm 32:8 states, *"The Lord says, 'I will guide you along the best pathway for your life. I will advise you and watch over you.'"* You can live a vibrant, fulfilling life through the help of God. Remember, God can always restore any and every aspect of your life!

Remain Prayerful

God's Word instructs you to pray without ceasing (I Thessalonians 5:17). I touched on prayer earlier, and as a reminder, prayer serves as a healthy outlet. There is absolutely nothing you cannot share with God.

Prayer is the avenue in which you communicate with God and God communicates with you.

Prayer is the way God comforts you when you are hurting, discouraged, or unsure of what the future holds.

Prayer is the way God encourages you and lets you know He is always with you. The late Mother Teresa stated that prayer is placing ourselves in God's hands. As you move forward on your quest to gain a strong sense of self-love, you must maintain a consistent prayer life. As you witness God transforming your mind and heart, Satan is also taking note, and he will do anything to distract you and attempt to stop you from moving forward.

As God makes changes in your life, you must have an open and continual dialog with Him. Talking with God is not about using eloquent speech; talking with God is about being open and honest regarding your feelings and concerns. Prayer is the avenue in which you can express your thoughts, emotions, concerns, and fears as you journey through the process of transformation. Sometimes, prayer involves silence due to the inability to put all your feelings and emotions into words, but I promise you, God understands silence.

As you recognize and understand that you are a masterpiece, prayer will need to become a vital part of your life. Prayer helps in more ways than one, too.

Prayer will help you survive as a new creature.

Prayer will help you feel content with yourself.

Prayer will help you remain committed to yourself when you feel discouraged.

Prayer will remind you of God's unconditional love for you.

Prayer will help you realize there are no limitations with God.

Prayer will help you remain devoted to God during times of uncertainty.

When you feel like you are starting to slack in your prayer life, refer to I John 5:14, which states, *"And we are confident that he hears us whenever we ask for anything that pleases him."*

Moving Forward with Determination

Despite the challenges and setbacks you may face, do not allow your heart to turn cold or your feet to stray from the path God has assigned to your life. I love the story of Jesus healing a disabled man (Luke 5:17-20). In that story, Jesus was in the process of healing people. Others tried to get the paralyzed man before Jesus, but there were so many people, that they could not find a way to Jesus. So, they went on the roof and lowered the paralyzed man down through the ceiling. Jesus recognized the man's faith and healed him. Because the paralyzed man was determined to get before Jesus, his request was granted.

That level of persistence and faith is how you must move forward as a woman seeking change, success, and contentment in Christ. Let nothing or no one stop you from going before God and the throne of grace with your desires and goals. *Be determined to be successful.* Keep your faith in active mode. Do not become discouraged if one door closes because God has allowed that door to close. Again, more than likely, God has closed that door for better doors to open for you. When you become determined to have God guide your life, the only result will be success!

Moving Forward in Wisdom

God's Word states that a wise woman builds her house, but with her own hands, the foolish one tears her house down (Proverbs 14:1). As I grow and mature, one of my deepest prayers is that God gives me the wisdom I need to be a successful woman, wife, and mother. I have learned the hard way and suffered the results of making decisions based on my emotions and my own understanding. I have learned that emotional decision-making can be dangerous, bringing about undesirable results and consequences. You must think before you speak and take action.

The book of James is one of my favorite books of the Bible. The book of James is very practical, and it applies to any season in life. The book of James deals with trials and temptations and the importance of listening and applying the Word of God to your speech and your wisdom, to name a few. James 3 discusses two types of wisdom, earthly wisdom and heavenly wisdom: *"If you are wise and understand God's ways, prove it by living an honorable life, doing good works with the humility that comes from wisdom"* (James 3:13). That chapter also discusses that the wisdom that comes from God is pure, peaceful, gentle, and easy to please. This type of wisdom is fair and honest. People who are wise and live in a peaceful manner obtain blessings as a result. From time to time, you should ask yourself the following questions:

Am I furthering my goals or reaching higher stages in my life?

Am I continuously improving?

Am I developing in a direction more beneficial to the previous level of my life?

Am I truly progressing?

Hopefully, the answer to these questions is yes. However, if the answer is not yes, I revert to encouraging you to a self-evaluation. Ask God to reveal to you the factors that may be hindering you or slowing your progress.

Is it a career choice?

Is it a relationship?

Is it your health?

Seek Him to reveal the answers.

As you move forward in life, you will realize that you cannot lean on your own understanding. Proverbs 3:5 shares, *"Trust in the Lord with all your heart; do not depend on your own understanding."* I consider myself an intelligent woman, but my intelligence is no comparison to God's infinite wisdom. I am only a finite being. Gaining wisdom and instruction from God will allow doors to open for you. Ask God to take you to higher heights and deeper depths through wisdom. Recite this simple prayer, one that you may speak, daily. I feel a great sense of peace and strength when I recite this prayer, first thing in the morning:

Dear God, I thank you for allowing me to see another day. I ask that you guide me and direct my path as I go through my day. I ask that you give me the wisdom to handle situations, seen and unseen. I ask that you guide me in making the right decisions. I surrender to you, completely, as I begin this day. Continue to keep your loving arms around me. I ask all of these things in Jesus' name. Amen.

Moving Forward in Discipline

According to Hebrews 12:11, we do not enjoy discipline when we get it: "No discipline is enjoyable while it is happening – it's painful! But afterward there will be a peaceful harvest of right living for those who are trained this way." Discipline can be painful, uncomfortable, and unfamiliar, but after you learn your lesson, you will enjoy the peace that comes from doing what is right. Moving forward as a new creature will require discipline. Discipline results in the development or improvement of skills.

If you want to have a more effective prayer life, it will require discipline to spend time in conversation with God.

If you want to study your Bible consistently, it will take discipline to regularly read God's Word.

If you want to be a positive thinker, it will take discipline, consistently speaking and thinking positive thoughts.

Discipline will require sacrifice, too. You must work at moving forward, even when you do not feel the desire to do so. You must pray and read God's Word when you feel yourself deviating away from your path and goals at hand. God will never leave you; all you have to do is call out:

The temptations in your life are no different from what others experience. And God is faithful. He will not allow the temptations to be more than you can stand. When you are tempted, he will show you a way out so that you can endure (1 Corinthians 10:13).

Just as you must condition your mind for success, you must condition your mind to be disciplined, too. Remain focused on your goal by exercising self-discipline, asking God to give you the self-control and willpower to move forward.

Choosing Happiness

As you move forward, you will have to decide to be happy and remain happy. Life coach Valorie Burton stated that "happiness is subjective," meaning that no one can tell you your level of happiness. Only you can make that determination. Happiness begins with you. Do not rely on your spouse, children, parents, siblings, or friends to bring you happiness. Another individual cannot determine your level of joy and peace. Only you can make that determination.

If you allow sadness and unhappiness to dwell within, your growth will stunt, and you will not be able to move forward in life. You will remain stagnant; worse, you may regress. I used to believe that if I had such and such, I would be happy. I believed that certain circumstances, possessions, people, and situations would inevitably create happiness in my life. With time and maturity, I have learned that my happiness is not going to come from people, things, or circumstances.

Ask God to give you an action plan to turn your discontent into happiness. Recite these words as you seek God for an action plan:

Dear God, I desire to remain in Your Will. I pray that You place me in the right places, with the right people, at the right time. I ask that You direct me in making the right moves. I desire to hear Your voice and have Your guidance. I cannot successfully live this life without Your presence. I ask that You be with me in every aspect of my life. I ask these things in Jesus' name. Amen.

I encourage you to write this prayer out and place it where you will see it throughout the day, whether you place this prayer on a mirror, refrigerator door, car dashboard, or on your coffee table. The more you speak these words, the more you will feel them, believe them, and live them.

The ball is in your court. As you move forward, release anything or anyone that interferes with your happiness. You should feel joy and peace despite life's imperfections!

Never Give Up

While rebuilding your self-esteem and self-image, you may become frustrated or discouraged by what you consider a lack of progress. However, I want to remind you that transformation is a process. A total transformation will not occur in one day or one week. Change takes time. At times, you may be your worst critic or enemy, but remember to encourage yourself and never give up, even when life seems bleak. James 1:12 states that great blessings belong to those who are tempted and remain faithful. So, revert to your roots and stay planted in faith. God will see to it that you bloom.

Maintaining an attitude of persistence is imperative. Persistence is extremely important when self-doubt and frustration arise. I am a strong-willed woman, and when I put my mind to perform a task, I move on a mission. I have learned to channel my energy in a sensible yet highly motivated manner. When circumstances are unfavorable, I remember to persevere. Life can bring unexpected circumstances, but you must learn to roll with the punches, and when rolling with the punches seems difficult, pray. Focus on all that is well. Focus on the positive. Celebrate small victories. *Small victories lead to bigger triumphs.*

Sometimes, the path you envisioned for yourself is not always the path that God places in front of you, but try to embrace what God is allowing. God oversees your steps once you surrender to Him. Your role will be to follow where He leads you, which will require perseverance and persistence to remain on course. Perseverance, persistence, and determination will allow you to overcome the obstacles Satan may place in your path. Those traits will help you overcome obstacles such as self-doubt, criticism from others, fear of the unknown, discouragement due to your current state (if it is not where you desire to be), and so forth. Always remember that God has great things in store for you.

Moving Beyond Survival Mode

God does not intend for you only to survive. He has the desire for you to thrive. God's Word will remind you of His desire: *"Dear friend, I hope all is well with you and that you are as healthy in body as you are strong in spirit"* (3 John 1:2). His intention is not to see you go through the motions, but to see you prosper. At some point, I became tired of living in survival mode. I wanted so much more than what I was experiencing. I wanted much more than what I was feeling. I wanted to live my best life, and I recognized that He wants me to thrive as His masterpiece.

You are unique in the eyes of God, and He has a unique plan for your life. Regardless of age or season, if you have breath in your body, God's unique plan for your life will continue to unfold. There are differences among every woman, but you have the same opportunity to thrive as anyone else. God's plan for your life is not intended to be compared to another woman's life or plan. Avoid pity parties because the more you entertain a pity party, the longer you will remain in that frame mind and the bigger your pity party of one will become. Do not live based on feelings and emotions. As women, we can experience a wide range of emotions in one day, particularly as our bodies are preparing or have begun menstruation. Therefore, make certain you do not make decisions based upon fleeting feelings. You do not want to make a major change or decision when your emotions are erratic because that could bring about regret. Ask God to assist you in thinking rationally. Again, do not make any major changes or decisions when you are in an emotional state. Your flesh will lead you astray, but God's wisdom will lead you down the right path: *"Then you will experience God's peace, which exceeds anything we can understand. His peace will guard your hearts and minds as you live in Christ Jesus"* (Philippians 4:7).

Enjoy where you are in life while proceeding to your desired place. Get energized and excited about your life, and remain in that enthusiasm! Continue to invest time and effort into yourself to prosper. You are worth the investment!

An Unconditional Love

Agape love is the highest form of love and charity. Agape love is the love of God for man and of man for God. Agape love is selfless, sacrificial, unconditional love. *Everyone experiences agape love from God.* I hope you realize that you are included in everyone.

Experiencing God's unconditional love as you walk on your journey is an extraordinary blessing. Man will withhold love and affection based on what you may or may not do, what you may or may not say, and based on how well you perform or what you achieve. However, with God, it does not matter what you may have said, what you may have done, or how you view yourself. He is always waiting for you with open arms. When I finally understood and accepted that God loves me unconditionally, that understanding saved me and lifted me out of the dark places in my life.

Because of God's agape love, you can be happy and whole.

Because God loves you, unconditionally, you can love yourself unconditionally.

When you are lonely and discouraged and feel as though you want to throw in the towel, put a smile on your beautiful face, hold your head up high, and keep moving forward. Know that God loves you despite how you are feeling. Isaiah 41:10

provides instructions for when you feel lonely and discouraged,

Don't be afraid, for I am with you. Don't be discouraged, for I am your God. I will strengthen you and help you. I will hold you up with my victorious right hand.

No Limits

Moving forward will require you to take the limits off yourself and off of God. For most of my life, I lived in a box that I built around myself. I placed limitations on myself. These limitations were created out of fear, fear of being incompetent, fear of being ridiculed, and fear of failing. Unfortunately, I allowed those fears to paralyze me for many years. As a result, I missed many opportunities. Thankfully, God replaced fear with faith, and He allowed me to see all that could be possible for my life. Today, as I look in the mirror, I see myself as a Proverbs 31 woman. I see a leader. I see a woman of vision, and I see a woman of influence.

Who do you see when you look in the mirror?

Who is staring back at you?

The moment I realized there were no limitations for me with God on my side, I began to venture out into new territory and explore different opportunities. As I age, I view my life through a different lens as opposed to my earlier years of womanhood. Not only do I see a masterpiece, but I see a kingdom woman staring back at me when I look in the mirror. Therefore, I have the authority and entitlement to live a remarkable life, all because I live according to God's standards which are found in His Word. As a kingdom woman, you have the privilege of dreaming big as you think, speak, and act according to His standards. As a kingdom woman, you can explore all God-given opportunities and options. God is bigger than anything that small minds could comprehend.

Celebrities have power and prestige because of fame and money. *You have power and prestige because of who you serve.* That statement does not derive from a position of arrogance or pride, but from confidence in God. God has continually proven His omnipotence. He continues to prove Himself, and I joyfully wait in expectation of what He has for me in the future. I encourage you to live in expectation of God's omnipotence, too.

Man has limitations; God does not.

Man has limited power; God has all the power.

Man makes mistakes; God is infallible.

The key to living your life without limitations and accessing all God has for you is to connect and remain connected to the vine, which is Jesus. The connection will be based on you seeking God through prayer and receiving and following the instructions found in His Word. You cannot produce good fruit without Him. If you remain connected to the vine, you have the right to live your life expecting no limitations: *"Yes, I am the vine; you are the branches. Those who remain in me, and I in them, will produce much fruit. For apart from me you can do nothing"* (John 15:5).

Your Complete Devotion

You must commit yourself to God as you transform, mentally, physically, emotionally, and spiritually.

Why?

Because as you commit yourself, your devotion to God will sustain you as you move forward as a woman with improved self-esteem and self-image. As a wife, I am completely devoted to my husband. As a mother, I am completely devoted to my daughter and son. As a woman, I remain completely devoted to God, and I nurture my relationship with Him. My devotion to God, my husband, and my children have improved my self-confidence and imparted belief in myself, which has significantly impacted my self-esteem and self-image.

Devotion is simply a profound dedication. Think for a moment. Are you truly and profoundly dedicated to God? The question is not to condemn you if you have allowed your responsibilities to take precedence over your relationship with God. My desire is to encourage you to evaluate where the nourishment of your relationship with God is on the spectrum of your life. Being completely devoted to God will allow you to remember you are a masterpiece despite circumstances or feelings. Devotion to God will also result in being able to more easily devote yourself to the important people and areas of your life. God cannot be last on this journey! God must be first. I have learned the hard way that it does not work in reverse order.

God does not want a portion of your being. He wants your entire being, and He deserves to have it all due to all He has done and continues to do for you. God wants to be involved in every aspect of your life. You cannot compartmentalize God. I do not function well without making time for God as my priority. I become easily discouraged, irritated, impatient, and mentally drained. As I mentioned earlier, people often experience a range of different emotions in the course of a day, but with the help of God and time spent with Him, you will feel emotionally and mentally sound to make decisions, continually elevating your self-esteem and self-assurance.

Give your all to God. In return, He will give His all to you. My former pastor once advised that we should give God 10% of our day and not our "trash time" or leftovers. I am more effective as a woman, wife, and mother when I give God the time He is due. Time with God allows me to remember who I am in Christ and who I was created to be in life. Just as your physical body needs proper, healthy nourishment to function at its best, so does your mind and spirit.

God's presence in your life will make the difference in how you view yourself as you move forward on the quest to feel and exhibit self-confidence. God helps you feel as though life is worth living. Profound dedication to God equals a life of success and happiness. Happiness, peace, contentment, and joy are fulfilled through God. Answers to life's issues as a woman, as His masterpiece, are fulfilled with God. God can and will fill the void in your heart when no one or nothing else can. It is never too late to recommit to God and spend time with Him. If you need to make changes in that area, take the first step to begin making the change by seeking counsel from a spiritual leader who can guide you in the steps of recommitment or attending a worship service or Bible study. I guarantee God will do His part when you do yours.

Walk in God Confidence

Philippians 3:3 is a wonderful reminder to take pride in Christ Jesus and Christ Jesus, only:

For we who worship by the Spirit of God are the ones who are truly circumcised. We rely on what Christ Jesus has done for us. We put no confidence in human effort.

There is no confidence in human effort. All of your confidence should stem from God and your relationship with Him.

Once, while waiting for my car to be serviced at the dealership, I was approached by one of the employees. As I sat in my usual spot, she walked up to me and said, "I always know it's you without seeing your face. You are always dressed so nicely, and you walk with such confidence." When she made that statement, I thanked her, but I thought to myself, "I do? That is the impression I give?" I appreciated the compliment, but the more I thought about her statement, I realized that she did not see the confidence I have in myself, but she saw the confidence I have in God. I walk with confidence because of who I am in Christ. The confidence I display is not the result of my accomplishments, but because I am a daughter of the most high God. I am a masterpiece! I am royalty. Therefore, I act like it, and I walk like I know who I am in Christ. I encourage you to do the same.

There is a significant difference between self-confidence and God confidence. Self-confidence is an assurance in one's judgment or ability. God confidence is having immovable, undeniable confidence in God's infinite wisdom and power. When you possess God confidence, you acknowledge that He and He alone are working in your life, on your behalf, and you are who you are because of Him. God confidence assists you in recognizing that He is the sustainer of your life, and He has all the knowledge regarding your innermost being. When you possess God confidence, you recognize that your trust is solely in Him.

You are capable of mistakes and downfalls, but God is infallible. If you are unable to think of any reason to place your total, everlasting confidence in God, reflect on His omnipotence. Beautiful woman, walk with your head held high and with confidence, God confidence!

"So we have not stopped praying for you since we have first heard about you. We ask God to give you complete knowledge of his will and to give you spiritual wisdom and understanding. Then the way you live will always honor and please the Lord, and your lives will produce every kind of good fruit. All the while, you will grow as you learn to know God better and better. We also pray that you will be strengthened with all his glorious power so you will have all the endurance and patience you need. May you be filled with

joy, always thanking the Father. He has enabled you to share in the inheritance that belongs to his people who live in the light."

(Colossians 1:9-12)

Conclusion

The information I have shared are experiences I have lived and, in some cases, continue to live. This book shared who I was and who I have become. By the grace of God, I am who I am. By the grace of God, you are who you are.

When I look in the mirror, I see a beautiful, intelligent, talented, God-fearing woman staring back at me.

I see God's masterpiece.

I see that I am fearfully and wonderfully made.

I see a unique woman with so many possibilities and opportunities to be all God created me to be in life.

When you look in the mirror, I hope you see that same woman glaring back at you with a smile.

My prayer is that this book has served as a tool in placing you on the right path to rebuilding your self-esteem and self-image. I pray this book gives hope to the woman who feels worthless and invaluable. I pray God gives you clarity regarding His plan for your life and who He created you to be. I pray God continues to reveal Himself in your life in miraculous and unimaginable ways. I pray you experience His presence in your life, every day.

I have great expectations as to how God will show up in your life. Prepare for greatness, bigger and better, and wide doors of opportunities that only God can mandate. Celebrate the woman you see in the mirror, flaws and all.

Love yourself as God's masterpiece.

As a woman thinketh, so is she!

Write your own prayer to reflect on, daily, as you move forward as God's masterpiece.

_____

_____

_____

_____

_____

_____

_____

_____

_____

_____

_____

_____

_____

_____

_____

_____

_____

_____

_____

_____

_____

_____

_____

Scriptures of Self-Worth

(New Living Translation)

"For I can do everything through Christ, who gives me strength."

(Philippians 4:13)

"Let all that I am wait quietly before God, for my hope is in him. He alone is my rock and my salvation, my fortress where I will not be shaken."

(Psalm 62:5-6)

"But the Lord said to Samuel, 'Don't judge by his appearance or height, for I have rejected him. The Lord doesn't see things the way you see them. People judge by outward appearance, but the Lord looks at the heart.'"

(I Samuel 16:7)

"You made all the delicate, inner parts of my body and knit me together in my mother's womb. Thank you for making me so wonderfully complex! Your workmanship is marvelous – how well I know it."

(Psalm 139:13-14)

"For we are God's masterpiece. He has created us anew in Christ Jesus, so we can do the good things he planned for us long ago."

(Ephesians 2:10)

"God dwells in that city; it cannot be destroyed. From the very break of day, God will protect it."

(Psalm 46:5)

"She is clothed with strength and dignity, and she laughs without fear of the future."

(Proverbs 31:25)

"You are altogether beautiful, my darling, beautiful in every way."

(Song of Solomon 4:7)

"But you are not like that, for you are a chosen people. You are royal priests, a holy nation, God's very own possession. As a result, you can show others the goodness of God, for he called you out of the darkness into his wonderful light."

(I Peter 2:9)

"'For I know the plans I have for you,' says the Lord. 'They are plans for good and not for disaster, to give you a future and a hope.'"

(Jeremiah 29:11)

Bibliography

Burton, Valerie. Successful Women Think Differently: *9 Habits to Make You Happier, Healthier, and More Resilient. Harvest House Publishers 2012.*

Maxwell, John C. How Successful People Grow: *15 Ways to Get Ahead in Life. Center Street Hatchette Book Group 2014.*

Meyer, Joyce. Battlefield of the Mind: *Winning the Battle in Your Mind. Faith Words Hatchette Book Group 1995.*

Warren, Kay. Sacred Privilege: *Your Life and Ministry as a Pastor's Wife. Revell 2017.*

About the Author

Lakeytha G. Clayton is a Licensed Master Social Worker in the state of Louisiana. She holds an associate degree in science, a bachelor's degree in social work, and a master's degree in social work. Lakeytha has worked as a social worker for the past 15 years in various healthcare settings. She currently serves alongside her husband who pastors at St. Luke Church of God in Christ in Baton Rouge, Louisiana. Lakeytha also serves in the Church of God in Christ as an evangelist missionary.

In April 2016, Lakeytha created a blog, www.Woman2WomanwithLakeytha.com, which serves as an avenue to minister, support, and encourage other women. She has the heart for women's ministry and being transparent regarding life experiences, struggles, and triumphs. Her sincerest desire is to assist women from all walks of life to reach their fullest potential in Christ. Lakeytha lives her life by the motto, *"God specializes in making the impossible possible!"*

Made in the USA
Columbia, SC
09 July 2024

38416912R00085